"What bold new voice is this? Iliana Regan is out to shake up the literary world in the same was she's shaken the culinary world. **Unexpected, flavorful, and distinctive,** *Burn the Place* is a debut to savor."
—**Beth Ann Fennelly, author of**
Heating & Cooling: 52 Micro-Memoirs

"Regan is amazing: Her exquisite Nordic-style cooking . . . is fascinating, beautiful, rustic and modern all at once."
—*Food & Wine*, **Best New Chefs, 2016**

"A chef-savant unlike any other in the U.S." —*Eater*

"One of the most creatively distinctive chefs of her generation."
—*Esquire*

"Queen of Midwestern Cuisine . . . Iliana Regan is upending how America thinks about the region's food."—*Chicago* **magazine**

"The only magical realist chef." —**Mike Sula**

"Iliana Regan is Alice. The fields and farms where she forages for ingredients comprise her Wonderland. We are along for the ride, and it behooves us not to be late." —*Chicago Tribune*

"Rarely is the importance of a clear visual aesthetic as obvious as it is in the case of Regan's food. Texture, dimension, color, and framing all come together in the service of some strikingly pretty plates." —*Chicago Reader*

Burn
the
Place

Burn
the
Place

a memoir

Iliana
Regan

MIDWAY

AN AGATE IMPRINT

CHICAGO

This book is written to the best of my recollection. Some names have been changed to ensure the privacy of those individuals involved. Some events have been pushed together or rearranged to move the memoir from beginning to end. Many important people and events have been left out, not on purpose, but because the story, at the time of writing, didn't call for them. Maybe there will be another memoir in the future to include all the things I left out.

First edition published July 2019

Printed in the United States of America

10 9 8 7 6 5 4 3 2 1 19 20 21 23 24

Cover design by Morgan Krehbiel
Cover illustrations: iStock/THEPALMER
Author photo by Jeffrey Marini

Library of Congress Cataloging-in-Publication Data
Names: Regan, Iliana, 1979- author.
Title: Burn the place / Iliana Regan.
Description: Chicago : Midway Books, an Agate Imprint, [2019].
Identifiers: LCCN 2018059694 (print) | LCCN 2018061002 (ebook) | ISBN 9781572848269 (e-book) | ISBN 157284826X (e-book) | ISBN 9781572842670 (hardcover) | ISBN 1572842679 (hardcover) | ISBN 9781572848269 (ebook) | ISBN 157284826X (ebook)
Subjects: LCSH: Regan, Iliana, 1979- | Cooks--United States--Biography. | Restaurateurs--United States--Biography.
Classification: LCC TX649.R44 (ebook) | LCC TX649.R44 A3 2019 (print) | DDC 641.5092 [B] --dc23
LC record available at https://lccn.loc.gov/2018059694

Midway Books is an imprint of Agate Publishing. Agate books are available in bulk at discount prices. For more information, visit agatepublishing.com

To my beautiful wife, family, and dogs, who love me for all of my contrasts, both external and internal.

And to my sister, Elizabeth aka Bunny, and her daughters. They all shaped me.

Prologue
Living the Dream

IT'S SATURDAY NIGHT. THE LAST NIGHT OF OUR WORK-week. We've shut down and a few of my employees are gone. A few are still inside. I pull the gate shut and lock it. I'm too tired to care. I'm completely over all of it. It's late now; the moon is bright and casts my shadow against the door. They realize I'm finally doing it. I hear them screaming like in some post-apocalyptic movie where I'm only allowed to save myself, maybe one other, but the rest we have to let die.

I listen. It's pathetic, really. The red tank of gas gurgles as I pour its contents over everything—the doors, the walls, the garbage container where the gas line runs up the side of the building. My hands shake, my gut drops, and my head, oh dear, my head. My fucking head. Obsessively I recall every time I've had to repeat myself, every time they don't listen, every time they fuck something up, every time I just have to do everything MY. GOD. DAMN. SELF.

"Fuck you!" I scream.

I want to take out the whole fucking block. I light a cigarette and get in my truck. I sit there for a minute and suck hard. The smoke enters my lungs and it hurts, but I like it. It's a good hurt, like I know I'm doing something bad, something that could kill me or will.

The smoke blurs my vision as I slowly let it seep from my mouth. I step out of myself, objective for a moment, and think, *Do I want this? Do I want to change my mind?* But I don't.

I pull away and with a flick of the butt, it's all gone.

Part One

Chapter 1
The Farmhouse

IN THE SUMMER OF 1983, I TURNED FOUR AND LEARNED a whole lot. For starters, I found out I wasn't a boy.

I sat at the top of the creaky stairs of our old farmhouse. I traced my finger along the wall, outlining invisible unicorns. I'd already gotten in trouble twice for using crayons. My sister ran up the stairs, naked beneath her robe. Nina was seventeen. I pointed at her boobs.

"Am I going to get those when I get big?"

"Yes."

She sat next to me at the top of the stairs.

"But why? I don't want them."

"Because you are a girl." It hurt my ears. I felt ashamed. Why was I a girl?

"But I don't want to be a girl," I said. Often I prayed at night for God to make me a boy.

"Sometimes you don't have choices."

Nina might have been my first girl crush, what with my being so young and not really understanding then what a sister was.

After she got ready, she left. My parents distracted me whenever Nina left the farmhouse. If I had to witness it, pure agony followed, as if the bogey monster was biting off my fingers, one by one.

On the morning of my fourth birthday, I used thumbtacks to pin a sun-faded and threadbare tablecloth over the picnic table.

The pig was already speared and spinning over charcoal embers in our driveway. My dad roasted all the animals out there in what looked like a big silver box with a chain on the side. That's what made the animal slowly spin. He was proud of that box because he'd built it.

Nina and I had bopped up and down in the back of the pickup truck going down Randolph Street to Mr. Elich's farm when we'd gotten the pig. Mr. Elich had little minks in boxes that I liked to look at, but he used those for fur. Nina liked his goats. She always liked goats. She used to show them in 4-H. But we never ate the goats.

Sometimes we had our own pigs to roast. One time my dad brought baby pigs home that he said must have been strays because he found them in the middle of the road, their baby eyes shining in the Oldsmobile's headlights. We kept them in the garage for a while before we penned them in the pole barn. The runt had hemorrhoids. Each night we went out there to rub cream on its butt. I remember

squeezing the tube into my dad's hand while he held the pig between his knees. When the pigs grew up, my dad shot them. I knew he would eventually. He held his shotgun and laughed as he walked out the back door. I ran to my room and buried my head beneath my pillows. I could still hear the pop and echo of the gun firing. The pigs had a good life and a good death.

Extraterrestrials might have planted me in our garden like the corn, growing up wily among the squash vines and beans. The farm was my identity even before I understood what my identity was.

The farmhouse was like a lot of farmhouses, I imagine. I was in love with that place. Everything about it was outrageously enchanting. It was in that house I cooked my first chanterelles, gathered from my grandfather's farm. I stood on a footstool and stirred in the butter. My mom and I added salt and pepper. The earthy aroma filled my sense memory. I never forgot. This is the house where I would thumb through *Gourmet* magazine while I sat over our heat vents in the winter. One time, I came across a beautiful picture of fresh pasta and marinara. It was summer, finally, and warm. My mom and I recreated it with her canned tomatoes. People always ask where I went to culinary school; it was in that farmhouse I learned everything I needed to know.

My mom stood in silhouette with the sun behind her. She had four bowls in front of her. They were clear, and each ingredient was so perfect: yellow egg yolks, flour, milk, green-tinted olive oil.

She poured the flour out onto the table, then pressed the bottom of the bowl into the flour and created a well. Her hands seemed big and old, but they weren't much older than mine are now. Her wedding ring seemed so big and thick; it just looked bothersome. She poured the egg yolks, milk, and olive oil into the well of flour. She dipped the tongs of a fork into each yolk, and one by one they began to gush bright yellow, almost orange. Carefully, she pulled the wet ingredients through the flour, incorporating a little at a time in a circular motion. After a few minutes, the middle turned from wet to pasty, and then shaggy. She pulled up the fork and ran her fingers over the tongs, loosening the clumps of flour.

At this point, I got really interested. Things got visceral. She plunged her hands into what was now dough and began to fold it over and over onto itself. Little by little, the flour on the cutting board disappeared into the ball beneath her hands. Like a little yellow sun beneath her palms. Supple. I got closer. It was aromatic. I fell in love.

After she put it through the pasta dye, which turned it to spaghetti strands, she draped the strands over a rack and set them on the back porch, saying, "This will help them dry." Back in the kitchen, I helped her chop warm tomatoes and herbs we'd collected from the garden. She dropped the tomatoes and herbs in a lightly oiled cast iron with crushed garlic and sprinkled salt over the top. I don't think she cooked them much—just warmed them, really. She cracked black pepper over the top.

She dropped the pasta into a pot of heavily salted water. "Fresh pasta doesn't take long," she said, then spooned up a strand and gave it a little pinch. "It's done." She handed me

the noodle and I ate it. She strained the pasta, lightly oiled it, added it to the pan with the tomatoes, and mixed it quickly. Then she turned it out into two bowls for us.

"Are you going to eat the tomatoes?" she asked me, because I didn't usually like tomatoes.

"Like this, I am."

This was how I learned to cook. I'm always asked this and truly, this was the start.

The house was old. The basement was often full of water and the furnace was fueled by lumber. I went down there in the winter with my dad and handed him the logs. I remember the red, splintering logs and floating ashes, wearing my dad's rubber boots and his old coat, which brushed the ground. My mom is still mad at my dad for that basement and "having to wash his underwear in water up to my knees for years."

The house was two stories. Some of it was gray brick and some of it was wood. My dad said he did a lot of fixing it up, as it "even had dirt floors in the bedrooms." Some rooms had electricity, and some didn't. Mine didn't till I was five or six. Lots of nights, I slept in my mom's room with her or on the living room floor with my dad. The floors in my room were plywood. I remember the day my uncle put the electricity in and I got carpet. My vocabulary became larger with all sorts of "what's its" and "fuck its."

I adored the wallpaper in the kitchen. It was tan and printed with images of old-fashioned kitchen whisks, bowls, presses, cranks, and dough-makers. The countertops were orange and the cabinets were dark brown. The refrigerator,

of course, was avocado green. Inside you'd find pigs' feet, sauerkraut, headcheese, milk, butter, rendered fat, pickles, and mushrooms my dad grew in the horse's manure out in the barn.

Underneath the cutting board island was a cabinet of cookbooks: *The Art of Orient, Dim Sum, Italian Cooking,* even *Larousse Gastronomique.* I don't recall my mom ever turning to these books, but occasionally, when I was inspired after watching an episode of *Yan Can Cook* or *The Frugal Gourmet,* I'd take them out and ask my mom to attempt something. She did, but her fried rice never tasted like the fried rice at Wah Yuen, a Chinese restaurant in nearby Merrillville.

This farmhouse was dropped smack in the middle of ten acres of cornfields, wild edibles, and Native American burial grounds with pulsating ghosts. A few miles beyond were Deep River and an old gristmill. The closest restaurant, the Beer Barrel, was another couple miles. All week long the sign read, "Tonight's Special: Fried Frog Legs." Everything was miles.

We had two gardens, one for vegetables and one for berries and herbs. Mom told me, "Soon as you could walk, each morning you'd run out the door, still in your diaper, and pull every single red raspberry from the bush." She laughed, and I saw that she could still see me in her mind's eye: "And I was always so amazed you already knew which ones were the sweetest and ripest."

The vegetable garden was carpeted with squash—big orange blooms hanging every which way—rows of corn, pumpkins, beans, peppers, and cucumbers. Name it and Dad was trying to grow it. There were all sorts of trees like

apple, pear, mulberry, cherry, and rows of pine. There were shrubs of elderberries and peonies. Where our hedgerow met the road, we had wild hazelnuts and crab apples. We had everything one could wish to eat from the earth, right there in that boring red state of Indiana.

We had a pole barn and chickens. There were a few pigs and a horse, April, and a pony, Smoky, who limped on a crooked hoof. I fed April apples; I don't know the variety, but I feel I can still smell them at some of the farmers markets— they were little mangled-looking ones, the kind that people pass up. I fed Smoky bouquets of purple clovers.

The pole barn contained rusted farm equipment and stalls for April and Smoky. There was a St. Bernard named George, who was many times the size of me. There was a commercial-size refrigerator, a freezer, and a big smoker. Those were from Jenny's, my grandmother's Polish restaurant. My dad hung beef to dry from the ceiling rafters. Right there in front of everything was a big hook from which you could hang animal carcasses to butcher or to skin. I liked to watch him. He'd back up the truck and unload the animal, tie its back legs together above the hooves, and up it went. He'd slice its throat and belly. There'd be a bucket underneath to catch the blood and guts.

The barn was so full of things. Dad liked to keep Hills Bros. Coffee cans full of gadgets, tools, and tool parts. There were tables stacked with machines, and then there were machines with still other things stacked on top of them. There was a broken drum set. An old piano. Everything was covered in dust. Going in a bit farther, you could make out a broken-down shark-tailed Chevy, light blue, from

BURN THE PLACE

some time in the '50s. I'd always wished we could ride in it. I loved to climb in and pretend I was on dates. I had seen my sisters with their dates, and I imagined a girl next to me, holding my hand. Sometimes I'd lean over and give her a kiss on the cheek.

A set of stairs led to the barn attic. Some steps were missing, and I was often reminded not to climb them, so of course I did. During kitten season I walked quietly around our property listening for their tiny hunger screams. I would find litters, lots of times up in the barn attic. When you got up there and sat at the top step, the daylight climbed in from broken slats in the roof and shone on layers of dust over dining room tables and chairs that had been retired from Jenny's. I sat there, baby kitten in my lap, and wondered about that lost time and place.

Not long before my birthday, we were all in the station wagon, headed home from the hospital. My mom and dad in the front. My sisters lined up along the back. While they didn't all live at home anymore, they were all there that day. I was lying across their laps. The doctors had broken my fever, but it was still coming down when they released me from the hospital. They told my parents to keep me out of the sun for a while and then that I should wear a white hat.

The station wagon was way older than me. Maybe even older than my sisters. In 1983, Elizabeth—Bunny—was twenty, Kelley was nineteen, and Nina was seventeen. It was warm that day, sometime in late July. I was still hallucinatory from the fever, almost dreaming, barely awake.

10

They kept talking, maybe to keep me present. They'd been instructed to get me into bed when I got home and to drape cool, wet towels over me.

A few weeks before, they'd said that for my fourth birthday we'd have a roast pig and clowns and chocolate ice cream. All those images spun through my brain, like I could see and taste them. I repeated the words without speaking: *Pig on a spit. Clowns and magic tricks. Chocolate ice cream.* I had this idea I wanted a white oxford shirt. I thought I could button it all the way up and wear a tie, and if I did that, people might think I was a boy. Then I could wear Dad's suit coat.

So that's what I did. My sister bought me the shirt as an early birthday present and then I put all the things on. I wore the white button-up, a tie that hit the ground, swim trunks, and the sport coat I'd pulled down from a hanger in my dad's closet, like a big blanket, and rolled the sleeves.

It was the middle of July and the heat was scorching. My mom was in the kitchen canning peaches. She wore a bandana to catch the sweat. Canning peaches in the summer makes things even warmer with all the boiling water, but it's worth it for the fragrance in the thick air. You become stickier with it, like you're sweating pectin. When I got outside, my dad was in the garden with a hoe: raising it up, then down, then dragging it, then back up again, like his arms were parts of a machine.

I went to the apple tree and sat beneath it. I emptied my coat pockets. There were my little green army men. I set them up in rows: the guys who were crawling, the guys on one knee, the guys carrying their guns above their heads as if they were treading through water. In my dad's coat pocket,

there was always a wad of toilet paper for blowing his nose. I had a pack of candy cigarettes my sister Elizabeth had purchased for me at the store. When we were in the car together, she let me light one with the car lighter when she lit her own filterless Camel. I put one in my mouth now and pretended to light it. I held out my hand in front of me like I was holding a beer. I cracked it open and took a big swill. I sat there in the shade of the apple tree and eventually fell asleep. Me, my GIs, my smokes, and my beer. Over time the sun shifted, and I was no longer shaded. When they found me, I had a sunburn on my head and I was sweating through the coat. I had fainted in the heat. That's how I ended up in the hospital.

I was good at being alone. I was afraid of humans.

On that small farm, among the bats, wasps, fireflies, and endless clouds, the stage was set for deep imaginings, escaping in daydreams so I didn't have to think. It was as if life happened inside a little box, and I was the marionette as well as the puppeteer. I felt like I knew more things about life than I should have. Like the universe was all those mason jars stacked in our pantry, and the world was just one of them, full of peaches.

On the day I began waiting for the mother ship to come take me back home, I was barefoot on the lawn, packing with a pair of socks in my undies. My little boy shorts bulged. I was shirtless and had on a tiny white baseball cap. I looked west; there were huge clouds forming across the sky, the sun was against my face, and I had the strangest feeling that I

didn't belong there. The expanse of the sky was so great; it occurred to me that there were many other versions of the world, many other versions of me. Maybe this explained why I heard so many voices in my head and had so many feelings about so many things. Many of my fears were based on that which had never happened to me but which I knew I had felt. Like drowning. Being locked away for murder. Running for my life. Getting kidnapped. Feeling like I was always being watched. Like I had done something wrong but wasn't sure what. Being tortured and murdered. Dying in a plane crash. Being eaten by sharks.

I had good imaginings too. I loved my family. The farmhouse was a hug. Thinking back to it, I feel it in my throat, emotion ready to burst. Baby animals were my thing. I found a nest of bunnies with no mom. I made a home for them in my room, bottle-fed them, nurtured them, and put them outside when they were big enough. Elizabeth helped me take care of a litter of kittens that was abandoned by its mother. I fed them fresh goat milk mixed with baby formula. When they were big enough, we set them free in our barn. Elizabeth kept one that was all gray. She had it until I was twenty. Almost until the day she died.

I think this can all be explained because of that sunstroke; maybe I suffered brain damage that day. As I slept, I imagined what it was like to die: lying flat with my arms and legs splayed out, rising up, like leaves picked up and twirling in a wind tunnel.

The thing is, I wasn't really made for this world.

My mom called me inside and I ditched the socks beneath the shrubs along the house. She had already filled the

tub. We didn't have a shower. Every bath for the entire family happened in that tub. It was small, made of baby blue enamel that was stained yellow from the well.

She used dish soap to create large mounds of bubbles; I could smell lemon and the chemical scent of pine. I took my He-Man and Skeletor action figures into the tub with me. Still worried about my sunstroke, my mom had drawn a cold bath. "When will school be over?" I asked.

"You haven't started yet." She looked at me a little quizzically and laughed.

"I don't want to talk to people."

"You're going to have to get over that. You can't go through life without talking to people."

I patted the bubbles around my face like a beard. "Is this like Santa Claus?" I asked.

"Yes," she said.

"Can I play football when I go to school?"

"No, they don't have football teams for girls."

I now very much disliked whoever "they" were. I didn't know why I was a girl, but I could still probably figure out how to play football.

"Can I do karate?"

"Maybe someday," she said and lifted my arm to scrub the dirt off my elbows.

My fourth birthday party, when it finally happened, a few weeks after my sunstroke, was as colorful as a pink sunset and had just as many layers. I'll skip most of it, but there was a good chunk where I disappeared to my room, overwhelmed

by the crowd. Lots of times, birthdays at our farmhouse were just as much for the adults as they were for the kids.

My sisters lured me out of hiding. They called me Lanie.

My sisters tell the story of that day best. Here's how they describe it (as told by all three):

Dad was sitting on his left leg, the other one hiked up. Over every bump, he howled about his hernia. It was like two socks filled with rocks on each side of his pants seam. Embarrassing as hell to see him sit down. We ate oil-soaked red peppers and garlic when we got to old man Elich's house. It smelled like manure everywhere. You'd have to be careful not to step in something terrible. Elizabeth was wearing sandals and we told her not to and she did anyway. She stepped right in horse shit. We went to the barn. His son was making blood sausage. There was blood everywhere.

Can't believe we used to eat the pigs from there. Everything was so filthy.

And do you remember what he smelled like?

Dad swears the pigs were OK, but we're surprised we didn't get some sort of disease.

He also had balls hanging down to his knees.

We cooked the pigs all the way. True.

We were stoned, anyway.

We got stoned in the barn back at the farmhouse with Tammy Demo and Barbie. Everyone came to the parties early. You remember Tammy's dark, curly hair? It was all in her face. She was more stoned than any of us. Dad had already put the pig on, and he and Rick

and Richard had set up chairs around it, like they were watching a damn football game. That's what regular dads did, but not hillbilly dads. Dad was a DP: displaced person. They watched pigs spin around on a spit. Talked about the crackle of the skin. We stopped by to pull a few pieces of the skin back to expose the flesh, which was slowly turning from pink to gray. We dipped the skin in salt and went on our way.

In the house, we made a peanut butter and jelly sandwich but only had two slices of bread. We cut it into thirds.

When we asked Tammy if she minded sharing, she ripped the paper plate into thirds. We laughed our fucking asses off.

When we didn't have anything to do, we invited the boys over. We told them to watch out for our dad, and to not smoke, and to definitely not drink around him. They got drunk and smoked anyway. They crawled out of Nina's window, which was on the second floor. It was right above the flat roof of the back porch. The boys were jumping off it into the deep end of the pool.

Lanie was quiet most of the day and disappeared like a bat out of hell when the clowns showed up. That was so funny. But it wasn't funny. She hid at most parties, even her own. We had to coax her out from her room with pig meat, bread, and green onions.

Lanie, why were you like that?

She was always like that. Never talked to anyone. Never looked at anyone. Remember how Mom had to order her food or talk to people for her until she was

about seven? Maybe first grade. In second grade, she maybe opened up a little.

I remember her hiding under the counter at Dairy Queen while an older grandpa-like man talked to us. Mandy was rambling on and on about sugar cones, waffle cones, crunchies. Lanie hung on to my leg and hid under the counter while we ordered. She wouldn't even tell us what she wanted, so we guessed: chocolate soft serve in a sugar cone with crunchies.

That was her fourth birthday. That was the day we broke Nina's nose with the skateboard.

By the end of the day, she took a picture with those clowns. Everyone took a picture with them; there were about thirty people. Those might have been the only clowns we met that weren't scary. Maybe it's different when it's two woman clowns. We asked them to be gentle with her and with the jokes, and they were.

That was also the night Dad chased Forest, Kelley's boyfriend, with the shotgun. There was a lot of commotion, him outside hollering about how they needed to get the hell off his property or he was going to hang and skin them in the barn. Do you think the boys we brought around were afraid of him?

Maybe. There was the time him and Rick Calous got in James Montgomery's car. James's hair was long, so they started putting their arms around him. One had scooted in from the passenger side and the other from the driver's. Then they started talking about how pretty he was and what a good kisser he might have been. James was definitely scared.

We grabbed Lanie and crawled out her bedroom window. We hid in the yard behind the pool's fence. We stood on some old railroad ties piled back there and just waited. Dad chased Forest all over the house and through the yard, and wherever they went, we went the opposite way. Forest got away 'cause Bunny was on the side of the house smoking a cigarette. It was dark out, probably 10 p.m. Dad says that when he saw her, he stopped dead in his tracks. Forest got away. He slung the shotgun over his shoulder, grabbed her by the ear, and dragged her into the house. Lanie was on Mom's lap in the living room. The lights were mostly off but for the kitchen light and upstairs light. Mom was sort of bouncing her on her knee. Dad says Lanie saved Bunny's life that day. He grabbed Bunny by the throat and pushed her against the wall, just beneath the stairs. He crumpled the pack of Camel cigarettes in his fist and put his fist up to her mouth. When he was about to shove them in, Lanie yelled for him to cut off her head and put it in the freezer. He fell to the ground, laughing. Bunny ran up the stairs. He couldn't contain himself. He figures it was because of all the animal heads he had in the freezer outside. She'd seen him behead things plenty of times.

Shit was weird at that house. It was also the best place on earth.

Chapter 2
Chanterelles

WHEN I WAS FIVE OR SO, YOU COULD HAVE SAID I was destined to be an alcoholic-transgender-trucker-carny. I slighted fate.

While I was still a bun in the oven, my family were all sure I'd come out with a penis. My name would be Brandon. Then there I was, kicking and screaming, a red prune-like mess of a baby, no penis. Whatever soul had crawled in and zipped itself up inside me was going to be scratching its way out for the next God-knows-how-long.

In the delivery room, my sisters screamed in unison, "Cheyenne!" I would be their little cowgirl. Polishing saddles and boots. But my parents chose Iliana, a vigilant, broad-chested Russian topped with a babushka—it was the name of one of my dad's ancestors.

My dad encouraged all of my boyish behaviors—hunting and fishing trips, tending to farm animals, sports, video games,

GI Joes. Maybe because he wanted a son, or maybe because my parents loved me so much they didn't care what others thought of them, he let me be exactly who I was.

On Route 30, west of the Beer Barrel, after the cornfields, was a shopping mall and a Burlington Coat Factory. These were a few of the big shopping centers near the farmhouse. I didn't like Burlington Coat Factory as much as I liked the shopping mall, because at the mall there was Hot Sam's, where you could get soft pretzels. There was also a coffee shop called Gloria Jean's, which smelled like vanilla, and a puppy store.

Once, my grandma picked up my mom and me for a trip to Burlington Coat Factory. When Mom was short on money, Grandma bought us things, but sometimes it meant we had to be abused while it happened. I wore cowboy boots and a flannel shirt tucked into jeans. And a yellow wig.

"Why's she got to wear that?" My grandma asked sharply. She wasn't soft, ever.

"I don't know," my mom said, "but she kicks and screams if she doesn't."

"Brat."

My grandmother always thought I was a brat. She had favorites, and I wasn't one of them. She wasn't terrible to me, but she wasn't nice. According to her, if you got what you needed and occasionally something you wanted, you were a brat; she hadn't had even the things she needed when she was a child. My grandmother was a bit over retirement age, but she worked overtime at the steel mill, driving a tractor. She didn't believe much in banks and hid her money all over her house. At one point, she had $20,000 inside a teddy bear she kept on her bed.

I still have a picture of my grandmother holding me on my first Christmas; I was four months old. My mom had dressed me in a red onesie with a little Santa cap. My grandmother's smile looks genuine. She loved babies. She had a warm heart, once you broke through her harsh outer iciness. She bitched a storm but still said yes when others were in need, like when my mom needed her to buy me new underwear and pajamas.

I was in the cart and my mother was pushing it. The fluorescent lights made everything look ugly. My grandmother pointed out the things I needed. Anything with pink or frills, and the answer from me was a violent headshake indicating no and tears in my eyes. We stopped at the underwear. Hanging in a row were three sets with Marvel superheroes printed on them, including one with the Hulk, my favorite.

I pointed and said, "I like it."

My mom said, "Those aren't for you." They were boys' briefs with the slit in the front.

"Sandra, if those are what she'll wear, then let her have them," my grandmother said.

Gritting her teeth, my mom replied, "Then you'll have to pay for the sex change when she's an adult."

I was a tomboy, plain and simple. I was also gay, though I was much too young to understand sexuality. I compared myself to my boy cousins—our baths together revealed the parts they had that I didn't. I vividly remember their little penis nubs floating around beneath the water where I had nothing. I was told that since I was a girl, I'd grow up like my sisters. I took baths with them too, noticing the parts I didn't yet have, like boobs. At the time, I didn't see boobs as

anything more than punching bags, and my sisters would yell for my mom to get me out of the tub. We grew up with one bathroom, no shower, and a small hot-water tank of well water; sometimes we took baths together, no matter the age difference or preference for privacy. I was curious why my sisters shaved their legs and wondered if someday I'd have a beard to shave. They explained I would not. Eventually, I began to pray for things: *Dear God, please let me grow a penis so I can be a boy.*

Still, my lack of a penis never stopped me from doing all the boy things. After a long school day during which I was forced to wear an itchy plaid skirt, I would change into a flannel and jeans, enter into the private world of my mind, and become the boy I wanted to be. Maybe if I had known then what kids know now, I might have changed my gender identity. I became acquainted with pretending; I projected the crushes I had on girls onto the boy double of me in my mind.

My father introduced me to his friends with a clap on my back and called me his "little boy." He likely said this as a joke, as my hair was generally worn short and tight, and you couldn't get me out of those flannels and jeans. I was proud of it, though. I'd wear a cowboy hat and tip it forward. *Yes, I'm his little boy,* I thought. But with all joking aside, my father taught me to love things usually reserved for little boys, like shooting a bow and arrow, learning to fire handguns, and tromping through the woods.

Once when he picked me up from basketball practice, he did something he had never done before and came all the way into the gym lobby. He had a tiny pig under each arm. I

was ecstatic. I wasn't going to live it down, though; the girls laughed and called me farm girl. We rode home in his small single-cab pickup truck, the tiny piglets secured in a box between us. The piglets had furry little heads. They were just about the cutest things I had ever seen. I named them and I loved them, and then he eventually killed them.

I didn't like that part, but it's just how it was. In the winter our barn doubled as my father's butcher shop. Animals were strung from the ceiling, their necks were sliced, and there were buckets beneath them to catch the blood. It was gruesome, but when it's your life, it's normal. There was always some run-in with death happening.

Once, I found a nest of abandoned baby bunnies and tried to nurse them. I put them in a box with lots of hay to keep them warm and fed them milk with a syringe. My mom discouraged this project. Maybe she knew it wouldn't have a happy ending, but she still let me take my chances. They didn't take to the milk and eventually became stiff and lifeless. It was devastating. In active contrast, I was equally fascinated with traps. I saw Elmer Fudd make a trap to catch Bugs Bunny and thought I could do the same. I wanted to make rabbit stew.

Another time, I found a nest of barn kittens. I was playing in our yard and heard little cries far off in the distance: *mep, mep*. I followed their sounds. I found the kittens and knew they must be hungry. Like a mad scientist, I got the syringe of milk. I had much more success with the baby kittens. I even found some of them homes. Then the reaper appeared again when one litter was attacked by Philip, our husky, who must have thought they were toys. He wasn't a mean dog, and I

never thought he intentionally tried to kill them. But when I got home from school and saw the blood smeared across his face, I ran to where I had left the kittens. They were thrown across the floor. Some were gutted, others had holes in their necks and were still gasping for breath. I grabbed Philip by the collar and punched him in the face and ran to my room. I did not emerge for several days.

Growing up on a farm taught me to be tough, no matter what. I learned about life and death fast. When dead animals sway from your barn rafters, when the heads and feet of the pigs you love end up in your refrigerator, and when every dog you ever owned somehow escapes through the back door and ends up flattened on Old Lincolnway, you learn death is natural.

Before I even knew what normal kids did, my dad buttoned me up in my little jean jacket, fit my knit stocking cap onto my head, and put a gun in my hands. He did this when the leaves were about golden to red and the sun was orange and the sky was pink. We were at my grandfather's farm, which was ten times the size of ours.

Rick, my dad's friend, had a belly that pushed out over his pants and threatened to break every last button on his flannel shirt. He had a beard and a red face, and a camouflage trucker hat he pulled low over his eyes. Rick sounded like he was drunk when he spoke, even when he wasn't drunk.

"Your boy's got a good shot," he said.

My dad chuckled. "He does," he replied and patted me on the head.

It was half past nine in the morning, and Rick was on his fourth cigarette and third beer. We had eaten breakfast

at a little diner down the road in Medaryville, which had a few dirt roads and a little town center back then. There was an A-frame post office where horses could be tied up outside. Medaryville wasn't cute, though. It was rough. People were poor. The houses had dirt floors, and many had outhouses instead of bathroom plumbing. There were wells and barrels of propane tanks in the backyards.

At the diner, I had scrambled eggs and two slices of bacon. I only ate the fat of the bacon, leaving all the strips of meat behind. The sun was bright, and it bounced in rapid geometric lines from one fork to another and into my dad's coffee. He drank his coffee black, and each time he sipped he made a large slurping noise. That mannerism irritated me. He also ate loudly by smacking his lips and talking with eggs in his mouth. Sometimes, even at the age of five, I had to slide down a seat or two for him to be out of earshot. I pretended I was playing on the stools rather than trying to conceal my irritation.

My grandfather's farm was one hundred acres of corn-fields, oaks, birch trees, ponds, abandoned cabins, sand, wild berries, and mushrooms and was nothing short of another universe full of magic. My dad's father, George, was hand-some and sweet. We drove up the side drive, past the house, and stopped just before the large barn and gate, which led back to the woods. The path to the woods was lined with wild blueberries and dewberries, and sometimes if I was there on Sundays after *The Lone Ranger* episodes, I'd walk the trail and pick them into a small basket. Then I'd retreat back to the porch, sit with the basket on my lap, and eat every single one.

George greeted us at the car. He opened the door, mostly excited to see me. He was taller than my dad. He was in his early sixties. I wouldn't have known it back then, but he was better-looking than most screen actors of his time. On Sundays he wore overalls and a white T-shirt. He was often on his tractor in the cornfield, and today he offered to let me drive it.

"They say there might be a storm today," he told us.

My dad looked up at the sky. I looked too. Aside from some big clouds and an occasional burst of wind, it seemed like any other day that we'd come out to visit.

"Yeah, I think they might be right," my father grunted. "We'll get moving."

Rick removed the cooler from the back seat. He lined the empty beer bottles along the fence just ahead of where the hedgerow met the cornfield. They took the guns from the trunk. Two rifles and one pearl-handled handgun. My dad checked the safety of the handgun and presented it to me, its iridescent handle glowing. My arm drooped with the weight of it. But I wanted to be strong—*little boys are strong*, so I'd have to be. I straightened back up. In 1984, it wasn't odd for a five-year-old to be holding a gun, especially in Medaryville, Indiana. But it might make someone look twice.

I put the gun down so my dad could show me how to make a triangle with my hands outstretched and how to close one eye after the other while looking through it. The eye that saw through the triangle without causing my hands to move was my shooting eye. He removed the safety and put the gun back in my hands. He wrapped his hands around mine and knelt behind me. He told me to begin to squeeze the trigger and breathe steadily. With his index finger over mine, he

pulled it back. He told me to aim at the bottle with my good eye, and when the trigger came all the way in, to breathe out. The crack of the bullet echoed as far as I could imagine. The bottle shattered. That day I proved to myself I could do anything any boy or dad could do.

"Your boy's got a good shot."

Maybe I could be a little boy, I thought. Soon, though, I'd be reminded of what it was like to be a pretty little girl.

My dad gave me a mesh sack for collecting chanterelles. We walked along the sandy path; it was lined with late summer berries about to drop. There was one ripe dewberry and I picked it.

"How'd you know that was still good?" my dad asked.

I smiled and shrugged, chewed, smashing every last seed between my teeth.

My dad kept his eyes lowered toward the ground. He scanned the landscape for chanterelles, which he said looked like orange flutes whose undersides had ridges rather than spores or gills. He told me I'd be good at finding the mushrooms because I was closer to the ground and my eyes were better than his.

My dad wore thick glasses, larger than his face, broken in the middle and held together by medical tape—cliché, but it's true. He was clumsy and nervous. He played out situations that could happen even if they had never happened before, like me getting lost or falling and breaking my leg. Or a hunter mistaking me for a deer and blowing me to pieces. All sorts of things that *could* happen, but the likelihood was slim.

I eventually inherited this trait.

My dad said the chanterelles would smell like the earth but would also taste sweet like apricots and spicy like peppercorns. I said these things quietly. Back to him and to myself. *Earth. Apricots.* I liked apricots. *Peppercorns.*

The leaves were wet, and the ground was uneven. A couple times I stumbled, but I quickly became oriented. I wanted to find the chanterelles so bad. My dad reminded me to stay close. I could see him out of the corner of my eye. Rick was a little ways ahead of us, and his black and red plaid jacket shone between the trees. The wind picked up, and what leaves weren't glued to one another from the previous day's rain blew around in cylinders then spun off between the trees.

When I stopped to tuck my lace into my shoe, as I was still inept at tying it myself, I knelt close to the ground and there it was, beautiful, orange, bright: a chanterelle. I knew it. My heart began to race as I looked farther out over the multicolored landscape and saw many more in succession, like soldiers marching toward me, dressed in orange uniforms, determined to battle. It was amazing. I gently cut them near the base with my pocket knife. For a kid, I had good hand and eye coordination. I collected them fast and kept going, farther and farther. I had already forgotten everything about staying close. I could faintly hear my dad and Rick talking somewhere, or maybe it was just the wind and leaves.

Then there were two boots, right in my path. They were big, connected to big legs in camouflage pants. After I stood up and tilted my head back to see who it was, I turned to run back to my dad. But Uncle Georgie had already picked me up by my waist. He held me up, the back of my head to his face. I could smell his sour breath, all alcohol and old

cigarettes. I silently began to cry. I didn't see my dad or Rick anywhere. I was too scared to yell or scream or even take a breath.

"I'll take you to your papa," he said. I didn't call my dad my papa.

Uncle Georgie was a Vietnam War vet. He made everyone uneasy. He was quick to snap from jolly to mad. When he came over to our house, I hid. He came over with his guns and would just shoot the air. The barn. Toward the house. My mom would yell at my dad to make him leave. My dad avoided confrontation at all cost, not necessarily for our safety but because he was so empathetic when it came to his brother. He would just look at my mom with pleading eyes: *Don't make me do this . . .*

He said he was going to take me to my dad, but he wasn't. He walked toward one of the dilapidated cabins in the middle of nowhere. There were one hundred acres. They were full of mystery and danger, like you could still see shadows of Native Americans and their horses; sometimes I thought I did, but no one else said they saw them. Someone like me could disappear there in the blink of an eye. Here he was, with his big arms wrapped around me. *I may never be found again.* He opened the door to the cabin and ducked beneath the threshold. Through the water-bowl of tears between my eyelashes, I saw Rick in his bright red and black jacket. I gasped for air. He was sitting on an old mattress near a potbelly stove, lighting a fire in it.

"Oh hey, George," Rick said. My uncle set me on the ground. Rick was rolling a cigarette, but he put it down to reach out to me and bring me closer to him. He put his arms

around me, but not in a scary way. He stood up and held his cigarette over the stove as if he were making s'mores, then took a long drag. He was the kind of guy you never saw blow the smoke out. He just kept it in his lungs somehow. Rick took my hand and led me out of the cabin. He brushed his shoulder hard into my uncle's chest on the way.

"I think your dad found some mushrooms," he said.

I didn't respond.

"I know George is scary, but you don't have to be afraid anymore. I'm here," Rick said.

Nobody would ever know Rick was a hero. I never told anyone what happened that morning. I never asked Rick why he was there, or if he knew Georgie was out there, or if he saw Georgie grab me. I was too young to think about that. Rick died a couple years later. And Uncle Georgie died not long after that.

I learned to avoid my dad's brother. For some reason, my dad could never see that he was harmful—maybe he just loved him too much. But Uncle Georgie made me fear for my life. He would grab me at family functions, just as he did in the woods, and whisper in my ear how pretty I was: *What a pretty little girl.*

That was the reminder. That was the difference. I knew what it felt like to be a little girl rather than the little boy my dad said I was.

"Where'd you go? Thought I lost you for a second." My dad looked a little panicked when we came up on him. Beads of sweat had formed beneath his hairline.

"Nope, right behind you," Rick assured him.

My dad proudly held his mesh sack before us. Through

the netting I could see and smell the mushrooms. It was like the afternoon sun right there in his hands. Suddenly a slice of wind jetted through the trees and sent Rick's hat flying. My dad stepped out into a clearing and gazed toward the sky. The wind shifted from warm to cold, then back to warm.

We began to run and as the wind grew stronger, I lurched forward beneath the weight of my dad's large hand over mine and struggled to stay with them. I felt like I was being pushed, or chased by a thousand ghosts, or maybe ghosts were running with me, brushing against me, trying to push me forward, over, out of the way. I imagined all the ghosts of Native Americans on their horses slicing through us. Rick stumbled, running as fast as he could, while I dragged behind my father. Suddenly my dad stopped, quickly buttoned the mushrooms inside my coat, then hoisted me onto his back. I wrapped my arms around his neck, and he held my legs as tight as possible. It was frightening and thrilling all at once. Here is where being afraid became fun. I'd recognize this feeling for many years to come.

We ran along the same path that always felt so peaceful when it was bathed in warm sunlight on Sundays when we picked berries. Now it was dangerous; the sand began to blow up around us. Rick charged like a football player as the sand cut around him every which way. My father ran in his wake, and I closed my eyes. When we got to the next clearing, the wind took my father to the ground. Rick slid beneath the car.

A large gray tunnel from the sky touched the ground at the horizon. The corn bent forward, as if bowing in prayer. My father reached for me behind him, but I had already been

picked up in a cyclone of sand. I was horizontal, rising up through the air, much the way I imagined how the aliens would take me, or how I imagined Jesus ascending to heaven in Easter Mass.

I don't remember all of this exactly. My memories are in large part informed by my father's telling of this story. I was picked up ten feet high, spinning in the sand. He ran after me, and about twenty feet away, I fell into a pile of hay at the base of an oak tree. He checked my head and felt my bones, and as the wind blew, he stretched out over me, pressing all his weight to hold me to the ground. He held on to the base of the tree. After about five minutes, the wind let up. The sky opened, and it began to rain. We hurried to the car and headed in the opposite direction from where the storm was traveling. We bounced over the gravel roads to Route 421 and headed back north. The car rocked along with the wind, but we felt safer, and Rick cracked a window and lit a cigarette. I rested my head against the cooler and clutched the bag of chanterelles inside my jean jacket. I ran my hand over the handle of the small pistol my father had taught me how to use.

My mother rushed to the car as we pulled up the driveway. She opened the car door before we even came to a full stop and swooped me into her arms. She knew something had happened, but she didn't know what. It was rare for my dad to be the calm one, but he assured her we were all fine. He avoided telling her about the sand tornado, and I avoided saying anything at all. Rick leaned against the car and opened another beer.

My dad gave Rick a look that said, *Time to go, man.*

Inside my mother changed me from my wet clothes

while I repeated what I had learned about the mushrooms: "They will smell like the earth but taste like apricots and be spicy like peppercorns." She listened. Moments like these made her stay with my father but also made her hate him just a little bit more.

In the kitchen, I dumped the chanterelles onto the table. *So many tiny flutes*, I thought. Most of them were still good; only a few were mangled by the storm. I picked pine needles from their stems and used a brush to remove the loamy soil from their ridges.

My dad trimmed the stems. He placed a large sauté pan on the stove and moved a little footstool in front of it. On the left side of the stove, he laid out butter, salt, pepper, old red wine, and thyme. The mushrooms were all neatly lined on a tray, three layers deep. He asked me to stand on the stool and gave me a spoon. He told me to take half the stick of butter and add it to the pan. Once it was melted and bubbling a little, we added the chanterelles. He added a few pinches of salt, and I did the same. We let the salt drop like rain. He told me to use the handle to move the pan over the flame and gently slide the mushrooms around in the pan. He told me to put the spoon under the mushrooms, lifting and turning them so they'd get lightly browned on all sides. He cracked the pepper over them and added in the thyme; I moved the pan back and forth and stirred the mushrooms. He put the bottle of red wine to my nose and told me to smell it. It was sour and pinched my insides. When we added a splash to the pan, the sweetness of the mushrooms wafted up and around us. I imagined I was a multitude of Russian nesting dolls made of mushrooms. We added another pat of butter and cut the

flame. I stirred the butter gently, until it was creamy. He put his finger in the sauce and tasted it; I did the same. He told me to add a couple more pinches of salt, and I did.

We spooned the mushrooms into three bowls, and he spread the table in the sunroom full of his larder: pickled pigs' feet, farmers cheese, beets and horseradish, peppers and tomatoes. He opened a can each of smoked oysters and sardines and placed the cans directly on the table, with forks resting alongside. My mom warmed bread she had baked that morning.

We sat down and ate a little of everything, combining the flavors and textures. The farmers cheese with the mushrooms. Swiping an oyster at the end of my fork through the creamy, buttery mushrooms. The tough meat of the pigs' feet with the gentle crunch of the sardine bones. The spicy beets and horseradish cleared my nose to welcome each bite of chanterelle.

This was the day I slighted fate and became a chef.

Chapter 3
Jenny's Café

A LONG TIME AGO, AS I SAT ON THE TOP STAIR TO OUR barn attic and marveled at all the restaurant furniture covered in years of dust, I saw everything I needed to see to know exactly what it was like. At Jenny's, I learned how to make pierogi through osmosis. I also learned how to quit something when I didn't like it.

I began my career at Jenny's Café.

Jenny's had closed before I was born, but I could see the dark wood-paneled walls and the light cast from thick, rust-colored fixtures over the tables. I saw the steelworkers, eating bowls of borscht, and sauerkraut and sausage on thick enamel plates, becoming heated behind their beer bottles and ranting about union dues. I saw my sisters there, in their Catholic schoolgirl uniforms, studying, restlessly shifting, poking at one another as the night grew on. I saw my grandfather kiss my grandmother next to the bar. I saw my uncle Georgie,

bouncing like a pinball between the tables as he drunkenly searched for the vodka bottle, hidden from him the night before. I saw my father bringing in a basket of green beans, corn, tomatoes, and zucchini from his garden. I saw him passing it to my mother through the kitchen window; I saw her smiling back at him. Sometimes, she really did love him.

Jenny is my dad's mother. My mom doesn't like her.

Jenny had five sons, and all five sons had wives. After my grandfather George died, Jenny couch-surfed, which created drama in her children's lives. Her daughters-in-law, all five of them, told one another of Jenny's mussings, about what she thought of the others. They gossiped, but she was mean to them. They felt it was within their rights to let each other know her thoughts. Combined, the wives were like *The Witches of Eastwick*. Then Jenny ended up in a tiny apartment in Hobart, Indiana.

My mom says I was an accident. She says we were all accidents. The first three accidents were all within four years. I came thirteen years after the last one. She says she found out she was pregnant with me after a night of heavy drinking, and when the doctor told her, she cried. He thought they were tears of joy, because that's how women were supposed to feel, but hers were more from helplessness, mixed with rage. By then, she had already built the case against my father. He was neglectful, mean-spirited, weak. He did his best to keep her dependent for years. He also made certain that she wouldn't think much of herself. She took care of her daughters. She cleaned the house. She polished the silver. She ironed sheets, babies' socks,

and underwear. She landscaped the yard, mowed the grass, watered the gardens, fed the horses, pulled the weeds, canned fruits and vegetables, saved seeds, and most importantly, she cooked. If she could, and she found ways, she drank to numb herself. Just a little, just enough to quiet things down.

She still can't really explain why she did so much because her own mother had never taught her how. She says all she wanted was a thank-you, someone to acknowledge how hard she worked—whether it was her husband, who didn't, or her own mother, which was never going to happen. At the very least, her mother-in-law could have thanked her for tending to her son's whims, being the head chef at Jenny's, and caring for her grandchildren. But nope.

There she was, apron tied around her waist, making pierogi, kielbasa, roast beef, fried chicken, hand-cut French fries, borscht, and deviled eggs. Her husband, vacant at best, was either in the mills or in his garden. And her mother-in-law was over her shoulder, criticizing her every move, from child rearing to pierogi stuffing.

My mom is a great cook. She comes by it naturally, and she is obsessed with it. My mom will be the first to tell you she has an eating disorder—then she will say it's just like how her daughter (me) is an alcoholic. So much for anonymity.

At a very young age, as she tells it, she found comfort in food. Food was love. Her mother was cold, her father was an alcoholic, and mostly she was left alone. Lots of parents tell stories about walking miles to school in the cold. In 1949, at five years old, in her dirty little dress with her messed-up

hair, no shoes, and a tiny bag with a pencil and piece of paper, my mom was put on a bicycle. Her mother pointed and said, "The school is that way." She'll tell it that she never had a birthday party until she was old enough to give herself one.

It was her Uncle Frank's fault. Occasionally, they would go to her grandfather's house, where Frank still lived. Maybe he was babysitting, because she doesn't remember her mother being around when it would happen, but Frank baked bread. He learned to bake in France and made big buttery loaves. He made firm, squat loaves full of seeds. Most importantly, he sweetened dough and fried it.

Frank cleaned my mom's face and hands, put her in fresher clothes, and brought her into the kitchen. She sat at a curved bench before a window with the small kitchen table before her. Frank stood on the other side of the table, a pile of flour between them.

Her grandfather's house was equipped with a potbelly stove that heated the room. Frank took a kettle of milk from the stovetop and motioned over it with his hand: "Not too much steam, you don't want it too hot." He spooned yeast into it and set it on the counter. My mother watched as it become foamy. He pulled a jar of flour and water from the top of the icebox.

"This is levain," he explained. "We will make a poolish so this bread will rise." The levain smelled like mushrooms, earth, yeast, and alcohol; it was interesting and sour.

She dipped her finger in and tasted it. "Mmm," she exclaimed.

"That's what gives bread the flavor you love so much," he told her.

They spent the afternoons together mixing dough and getting the kitchen as hot as possible. My mother helped roll out the bread. She pinched it closed before placing it in the long loaf pan, which she had smeared with butter. After Frank put it on top of the stove, she didn't move for two hours, until it was ready to bake. She read Archie cartoons and flipped through his cookbooks and recipe notes as she waited. Every couple of minutes, she looked up to see the level of the loaf because she knew that when it peeked from the top like a cloud, it was ready. Frank gave her mittens to wear while she put it in the oven. The hiss and crackle of the logs from inside the stove were the perfect accompaniment, especially when rain began to fall. When she got home that night, her mother would likely still be at work, and if or when she got home, she would still be cold and vacant. My mother would put herself to bed, lightly shivering until her body heat accumulated beneath the covers. She'd fall asleep dreaming about the day with Frank and the bread.

When he opened the oven, the champagne-like smell of yeast and caramelized butter permeated the room. So thick you could feel it on your skin. The sweet smell stuck in your hair for days.

"Can we cut it?" She asked this every time a loaf came out.

"No, we have to wait."

When they finally cut into a loaf, Frank had a method.

This is what my mother recalls in her daydreams, sleep dreams, and whenever she still tells this story. This is where the emotional exchange happens. This is how food becomes your comfort, your companion, your best friend.

Frank sliced the bread one hour after he pulled it from the oven. There'd still be a little steam from its insides. I know he didn't want to slice it yet, but he did it for me. He slathered it with the butter he'd made from churning the cream he bought from the farmers at the Fifth Avenue Sunday market. He'd leave that butter out for days. The fragrance became ripe, like a deeply marbled blue cheese. Then he coated all the butter with a thick layer of sugar. Then—the strangest part, that back then didn't seem strange at all—he poured a small amount of boiling water over it. Just slow enough to melt the sugar and butter right into the bread.

Frank would sit down next to her and for the rest of the day, she was allowed to eat as many pieces as she wanted while they listened to the fire and the rain, if it was raining, and read the newspaper together.

This story starts to become my own with Club 57 in Gary, Indiana, back when the city was promising to become a metropolis. Theaters, dime stores, parks, the waterfront—everything was there, it had every potential to be Chicago's twin city. But the American dream would ultimately leave Gary a ghost of itself.

In the early '50s, Club 57 was *the thing*. This was when being a bartender was a very real job, and Frank was the best one in Gary, with his copper stirs, corkscrews, bottle openers, and sleeve garters. Everyone came to Club 57 on Fridays at 3 p.m. That's when Frank's shift started. My mom

went there too. After school she'd climb the long narrow staircase up to the second floor over the dime store. Short tables zig-zagged across the open room, and there were small metal chairs with red cushions. The floor tiles were black and white octagons and made you dizzy if you looked at them too long. At the far end of the room was a stage, where at that hour a band would be setting up. Occasionally, you'd hear banter, the ting of a cymbal, or the drawn-out, slurred speech of a customer.

Frank would make my mom a grenadine cocktail with a cherry, and she'd sit at the far end of the bar. Frank would put a bowl of beef and noodles in front of her and she'd devour it.

"Hungry kid," a guy at the bar would mention.

Frank would respond, proudly, "Yep."

Food was love for Frank too. He thought kids should be stocky. My mom had a round little baby face with big gray eyes, and her head had brown curls with hints of red, punching every which way. She typically wore a little white blouse, dingy at the collar, a small plaid skirt, and penny loafers from the previous year that made her toes curl toward the balls of her feet. As he filled her bowl a second time, Frank always reminded her she was a sweet girl and that he loved her.

"Those beef and noodles, though," my mom said, "were the best thing. They really drew a crowd, and in no time the whole place would be full and the band would start playing."

My mom usually fell asleep on a couch backstage and would wake up the next morning at her grandfather's to the smell of caramelized beef. Sleepily, she would wander into the kitchen, now dressed in one of Frank's buttoned work shirts, long as a dress. She rolled the sleeves what seemed

like a hundred times so her little hands could reach for the glass of milk he set on the counter for her. She sat down at the same table where they made their bread together.

"I got you something," Frank told her once.

"What?"

He began to unwrap what looked like a hunk of meat in butcher paper, tied up pretty with twine. When he turned around, he was holding a brand-new shiny pair of what looked like baby doll shoes.

My mother gasped. "Those are for me?"

"Yes," he said and began to slip them on her feet. She wiggled her toes inside of them.

"I can move my toes."

"I know," he said. "I saw you limping, and that's not right for a little girl who should be walking like a ballerina."

She hugged his waist tight.

"OK," he said and set her back down. "Let's get cooking. Time to make beef and noodles."

He turned the beef over and over in the pan until each side was equally dark brown and nearly charred at the corners. The meat had been dusted in flour that was now stuck to the bottom of the large Dutch oven, becoming darker and darker. He added his cultured butter and two onions, sliced thick, and two smashed cloves of garlic, still in the husk. Then he covered the meat with water. The bottom of the pan sizzled and popped and created large wafts of smoke and steam. He quickly put on the lid and added the pan to the oven.

Frank was French Canadian, with a strong aquiline nose, high cheekbones, bright green eyes, and silver hair pushed

high off his forehead. Frank was tall and not very beautiful, though his features were nice. Altogether he had a handsome quality, but you wouldn't have known it at first glance. It was his upbringing: everything was tough for his family. He'd seen it all: from cowboys, wagons, and dirt roads to shark-fin Chevys, steel mills, and smokestacks. He did everything to its fullest, no shortcuts, no tricks. Frank made everything from scratch. Frank milled his flour, churned his butter, baked his bread, and fermented the grapes from his backyard for wine.

"That's how it was," my mom said. "That's why it was always so damned good."

Frank gently opened the drawstrings of his flour sack and created a mound on the center of the table. The white dust spilled out and up into the air. It was beautiful, my mom thought, like a mini avalanche. He formed a well and had my mom crack a dozen eggs into it. Frank made his own crème fraîche by leaving cream in a jar on top of his icebox with the slightest dash of apple cider vinegar. He placed two large spoonfuls in the center of the well.

"Now mix it," he said and gestured for her to put her hands in and massage the dough. After she made a big, rag-like mess, Frank pulled it toward him and began to knead it on the table. He turned it over and over until it was uniform. He poked his finger into it and it slowly sprung back.

"Perfect," he exclaimed. He wrapped it snug with a kitchen towel. "Now we let this rest." He set it in a cool, dark corner on the kitchen counter.

Several hours, many crossword puzzles, and one coloring book later, Frank began to roll out the dough with a large rolling pin. Once he had nice thin layers, about an eighth of

an inch thick, he tossed the sheets to my mom. With steady concentration, she cut them the size of chewing gum sticks per Frank's instructions.

When Frank pulled off the Dutch oven lid, my mom felt what girls at school described they felt about boys they liked: her stomach felt full of butterflies and her heart felt like it was beating all the way up into her throat. The beef was brown and juicy; the muscle pieces began to fall away, held by a web of milky white fat. Frank explained that you should always cook with beef that has a good amount of fat between its muscles and, most importantly, cook it until it will fall apart—but not too long. Just until it's perfect.

He pulled the meat from the pan, into which he added a few more cups of water, some bay leaves, and a splash of red wine. With two forks he gently broke the meat into pieces. As the pan's contents came back to a boil, he showed Sandra Lee how to cook the noodles, right in the same pan. The flour from the noodles thickened the pan drippings, water, and wine into a thick gravy. Once the noodles were floating in the gurgling gravy mess, Frank added the meat back in and stirred. He used a big wooden ladle to heap the contents into a china bowl and placed the dish before her.

Frank was everything.

When it was 3 p.m. on a Friday at Jenny's, the pierogi were ready. The St. Andrew's church bells at Thirtieth and Broadway tolled, and a little farther down the way, the steelworkers filed out of the mills after their shifts, lunch pails empty and stomachs growling. Jenny's staff was hustling as the dinner

crowd began to assemble. There was my mom and her sous chefs, Kasia and Xena, who traveled on the South Shore Line from Hyde Park in Chicago. My dad's cousin, Mikey, who washed the dishes. Irene, the half-Japanese busgirl, who was very exotic to my family, along with Soo Young, a waitress who had married an American soldier during the Korean War. The token alcoholic of the family, my uncle Georgie, sat at the bar; my grandmother coddled him.

On a blackboard behind the bar, "Specials" was written large. Underneath, in his childlike scrawl, my dad wrote, "Pierogi." He was still in his stained jeans and work shirt from his shift at the mill.

"Sandie, what's the filling?" he asked.

She heard him but didn't respond. She was irritated, not only with him but with everything about him.

My mom directed Kasia and Xena to dust the long stainless-steel table with flour before placing the sheets of dough onto it. They had sheeted it with a hand crank. Once it was in place, they used small water glasses to cut out circles. They stacked the circles together. Once they were all cut, they began to fold them over a multitude of stuffings: potato and cheese, beet, blueberry jam and cheese, sauerkraut, and little sausage pieces. They passed these to my mother, who then tossed them into boiling water. Once they floated, she strained them. Then she added them to a hot cast-iron skillet foaming with butter. This went on all night. Sometimes they made over 1,200.

The pierogi at Jenny's Café were amazing. Everyone wanted them, and that almost made my mother more resentful. She felt trapped and made many promises to herself

to hit the road, leave my father, just get the hell out. In her mind, though, she didn't have anything—no money and no skills, though they were emanating from her. She had three daughters and another kid on the way. The disdain for my father took hold and, like a seed, rooted deeper each day.

At the end of her shift, my mother was sore. I was becoming heavier, and she was less energetic. She had to sit down while Xena and Kasia began to clean.

That's when it happened. That was the last day.

It was half past ten, and my mother was already thinking about her girls at home. Worried they were not in bed for school. Worried that they might be in trouble because they often were. By this time, Elizabeth had already proved to be just like Georgie. That's how it was: if you had the same problem as someone before you—alcoholism, depression, name it—you didn't call it what it was. You said, "You're like Georgie."

My mother twisted a part of her hair for comfort as she stared blankly out at the empty restaurant. The lights were dim. Irene and Soo Young counted their tips at the bar. She could hear their girlish whispers in the background. Suddenly, Jenny stepped into her line of vision.

My father was now in my grandmother's place, coddling his brother.

"What are you sitting for? Shouldn't you be cleaning? You're lazy." Jenny said this loud, so everyone could hear. Even Xena and Kasia looked through the round kitchen windows. My mother looked toward my father to say something, to bat his mother down, but he seemed to not hear. My mom slowly rose from the chair, belly first.

"Go fuck yourself."

Jenny immediately began to cry, as if my mom had hurt her feelings. "She's so mean," she said to my father, tattling like a child.

My father was irritated—not at my mother and not necessarily at his mother, but just that he had to be bothered with this in the first place.

That night, after everyone was gone, my mother posted a CLOSED sign on the door and she never came back. Jenny tried to operate without her, but she couldn't. Jenny tried to play chef, serving hot dogs and potato chips, but that's not what the people wanted. Within weeks, Jenny's was closed for good.

Chapter 4
Chinese Food

"THIS KITCHEN SMELLS LIKE A DIRTY VAGINA!"
I yelled at the top of my lungs. My sister used a nutcracker
against the shells of snow crab. My dad said snow crab has
a better flavor than king crab, but it's much more difficult to
get to the meat.

I was ten and 1989 was bangin' neon. I had no idea what
a dirty vagina smelled like, and the kitchen probably didn't
smell like one. I was showing off. Lisa was over. I saw her in
the living room, bent forward at the waist, laughing so hard
she was crying.

That year our farmhouse turned into a full-blown so-
rority. Well, not completely, but it was when all the women
who menstruated synced up and wreaked havoc. My mother
was in her forties, and my sisters were in their mid-twen-
ties. Elizabeth had moved back in. Kristina, my first niece
and to this day the cutest baby who ever lived, was eighteen

months old. Kelley had fought the last fight with her boy-friend, Forest, that she would ever have. He'd nearly choked her to death. She woke up on her kitchen floor after passing out. We were all on a collision course for the bathroom the day my mom announced her divorce.

By now, I had become a girl. I'd already had one boy-friend and we had talked on the phone every night, while *Wheel of Fortune* was playing on the television in our living room. Lisa, my best friend, had taught me how to do this girl thing. Lisa was a tomboy too, but she sometimes wore a sundress. She read books, she was pretty, and she was kinder than I could be. I looked up to her, was jealous of her, and wanted to be like her. She also taught me that being a girl wasn't that bad. My sister Nina had shown us how to tease our hair: while bending forward, we used the blow-dryer and hair spray together to create a massive windblown effect. We did this, and we looked cool. We wore fluorescent clothes and had big, thick, colorful eyeglasses. The truth is we were nerds. Sometimes we felt cool, and sometimes the popular boys liked us. They liked Lisa more. She was a good wing-man, and the ones she didn't like moved on to like me.

We played softball together and learned guitar. We bought each other Christmas and birthday presents. We laughed all the time, created dance routines to Disney movies (but not ones where any animals died), and the day I told her about my parents, she cried for me when I didn't know how to.

Nina was bent over, naked, creating her Mötley Crüe dance girl hairdo. I pulled down my pajama pants and sat on the

toilet to pee. Elizabeth was giving Kristina a bath, and Kelley was wiping her face with cotton balls when my mom came in, tired. At this time, Mom was large. I could barely touch my fingers together when my arms were wrapped around her. She was still lovely, though, at least to me. My friends all loved her black and white zebra-striped eyeglasses, but this morning she wasn't wearing them. She had gotten her teeth fixed a couple years prior; now when she smiled, instead of the sporadic holes that gave way to the back of her mouth, the bridge shined. She also did her hair in a way that girls and boys both wear today—shaved on one side and long to her chin on the other, dyed auburn.

I wouldn't have been able to tell from the looks of her if she'd been crying. I don't even know if my sisters already knew. When I finished peeing, I got up and put the seat down. We couldn't flush when the water was running, especially if the baby was in the tub.

"Your dad is moving out," she said, mostly looking at me. I quickly looked at my sisters to see if they had heard the same thing I had. They didn't stop what they were doing, but Nina stood up, her boobs spread to the sides. (I never ended up getting the boobs of any of my sisters. Maybe it was all the wishing to be a boy I had done.) I think she could see the panic in my eyes.

"I don't care," I said, turning my eyes to the floor. I couldn't process my thoughts quickly enough. *What would happen to us? Would we still live here? Why? They do fight all the time. Is that how this works?* My mom thought my dad was terribly annoying. You could hear her grunt every time he yelled, "Yello?" as he answered the phone. It was like every single

thing he did irritated her. *Was it because she didn't love him or he didn't love her? How would we afford to live?* My mom, as far as I knew, only ever had a few jobs. She had once cooked at Jenny's, and she had made macramé but not to sell, at least not anymore—it mostly twisted in the corners of our ceilings, holding her potted spider plants and jade plants. She had been our school cafeteria lunch lady, and she was great at organizing the fundraising carnival every summer, where she pumped out elephant ears from our church's basement. She and Otto's mom, Mrs. Shragel, catered weddings and a few other events from the cafeteria's kitchen, but that was it. I wasn't sure how any of those things were going to support us.

I was worried. I didn't know what would happen. I didn't want to move from our house. That would be too much for me to handle. It was everything to me; it was almost close to the feeling one might have about God.

This all happened in early July of 1989. Lisa and I played softball that summer. I was shortstop, and she played first base. Her giraffe-like stature allowed her to reach farther than any of the rest of us; she'd throw out her arm in whatever direction the ball was coming from and *bam*, it'd land right in her mitt. We had lots of practice playing catch in our yards, and she was good. I would have never admitted it then, but she was way better than me. Though I was a decent enough shortstop when I applied myself. I could dive for the balls and whip them to her before the player reached first base. I could size them up while they were on deck: chunky,

I had time; stocky, might be a fly ball, easy to catch; fit, might be a grounder, so I got low; lanky, likely to miss.

Lisa wasn't good at bat. Sometimes she played catcher, which she was good at, but once she ended up getting her elbow clocked hard when she'd stuck her long arm out too far. She fell to the ground and began crying her eyes out. I ran to her, held her head as she wept, and then her mother scooped her up. Nothing was broken, and she didn't have to go to the hospital, but that's how those things are—the funny bone gets hit and it's not fucking funny at all.

The night Lisa's elbow got hit, I lay in bed staring at my ceiling. I was thinking about my parents. I could hear the night train on the tracks from about a mile away. The crickets and cicadas were louder than usual, and it seemed to be getting more humid as each minute passed. My stuffed animal Ewok was at the end of the bed; I sat up and brought him closer to me. I felt alone, which was not unusual. I could hear what sounded like Bunny pacing back and forth downstairs. I imagined Kristina in her arms.

When I couldn't hear anything anymore, I got up and crawled through my bedroom window. My room was on the second floor and my window opened onto the roof. I hung from the gutter and lowered myself onto our picnic table. The next day was the Fourth of July. We were going to have our party, as planned. My dad would roast the lamb, but he'd be quiet except for occasional whispers to the guys or a joke at my mother's expense—as if she wasn't hurt enough. My mother, on the other hand, would indulge in Miller Lite, maintain a steady buzz. She'd convince herself we'd all be fine and tell us how she wanted to take a crash

course in phlebotomy. She'd explain the new diet she would begin maintaining, as of that day. She wouldn't touch any of the food, and she'd prepared quite a bit, but would instead make herself a cucumber and tomato salad. She'd describe to everyone what feta cheese was and how she had discovered it at a little Greek store at the edge of Gary and Merrillville. *You can't see it from the road and unless you take a wrong turn, will probably never find it.*

I got on my bike with a little pillowcase sack containing my eyeglass case, mitt, and Ewok over my shoulder. As I rode across our gravel driveway, I looked back at the house once more; it was completely still and dark. I was afraid to ride in the dark, but I also liked the idea of sneaking out of my house and riding farther than I was allowed even during daylight hours. I wanted to check on Lisa, and I felt lost.

I threw a couple of pebbles at her window. I could see the tiny glow of a yellow light. It wasn't that late, just 10 p.m. The rest of her house looked dark. She peeked out.

"Can you let me in?"

"Yes, just a moment." Lisa had a way of speaking like an adult.

We sat on her bed in the soft glow of her reading light. We talked about her elbow for a minute, and then I said what I realized I'd come to say.

"My parents are getting divorced." I turned my eyes down to her Care Bear bedspread. My feelings were caught in my throat, stuck there like a rock, along with my heart, which I imagined fragmented into pieces. I could feel Lisa looking at me, and she began to cry—the tiniest splatter of tears hit her knees. I scooted closer to her and, as I knew she would, she

embraced me, and we lay down together. I was careful not to bump her elbow, and she kept it out of the way, thrown over my chest. She wept, holding me, and I stared up at the ceiling. My throat expanded, but I could not let my feelings escape. I was afraid of crying. Maybe that's what Lisa was doing. Crying because I could not.

Even though it seemed everything would soon be in shambles, that summer wasn't half bad. There was a drought, too, and our well water was more yellow-hued than I could remember it being before. Nina brought home lemon Kool-Aid and mixed it in her shampoo. She said it got the rust color out of her hair. I only noticed the bathtub was sticky and her hair looked brittle. But our houseful of women just kept on going.

August was hotter than hell. At night I lay in bed, as still as possible. When I complained about being too hot, my mom told me not to move. "Just lie still," she said. "The more you move, the more your body heats up, and you sweat."

She was going through menopause. When my sisters were mad at her, they told her, "Take your meds." My dad was already gone. He moved out soon after the Fourth, not long after my mom told us; it was clear they had all known about the divorce for much longer than I had—though I didn't put that together until I was a teenager.

Kelley was pretty quiet and got a VCR for us, so that was cool. We watched movies in bed and ate popcorn my mom made on the stove.

Nina and Bunny fought. Not just arguments but real fights—they threw punches and pulled each other's hair.

Nina had a great selection of clothes—fringe, leather, jeans, silk, linen, in all the colors. Purses, jackets, shirts, skirts, dresses, handbags, chaps—whatever you could wear or add as an accessory, she had it. Nina's room was dark even though it faced south; she kept the curtains drawn. Her mattress was on the floor, and she made her bed every day. Her room was all shades of brown, and she was still sort of a cowgirl. She polished her shoes and leather boots with saddle soap. She polished April's saddle once a month. But she hadn't used a saddle in years, as far as I knew. She rode bareback, and when she emerged from the barn on April, her thighs gripped the horse's ribs.

Nina's closet was organized from thinnest and lightest to heaviest and darkest. Even if you were careful to remove the hanger along with the shirt that you took, she always knew; if something was gone, it was as if it threw her operating system out of whack. I suppose that's obsessive-compulsive disorder. She also made sure our rugs were straight and the carpets were vacuumed in a certain direction. I learned to get on my hands and knees as soon as I entered the hall; I crawled backward to my room and, with my hands, pushed the carpet in the direction she preferred.

It's statistically proven that crime goes up during summer. The heat changes something in us, makes us more edgy. Nina was already pissed when she got home from work. She was an EMT and had worked overtime making 911 calls. She wore her full uniform: a dark navy shirt, buttoned and stiff-collared, tucked into thick polyester pants held up by a

heavy belt. The pants were tucked into her socks, which just barely rose above the tops of her combat boots.

It was ten at night. The last lights were about to go out in the house. My mom had snuffed out her last cigarette and was getting ready to put Kristina to bed. Kelley was sleeping. Bunny had not been home for what was going on thirty-six hours.

Nina had gone up to her room, but within minutes she came racing back down the stairs. "She got one of my fucking shirts again!"

My mom quickly put Kristina to bed and shut the door. She attempted to calm Nina, but she was already pretty far gone. I knew how this was going to end. Through the large picture window in our living room, headlights turned up into our driveway. *Shoot*, I thought. I knew it was all going to collide. In a few short moments, the roof was going to blow off the house.

Nina paced by the back door. I crawled up on the counter by the kitchen sink and watched through the window as Bunny got out of the car. The moon was out and the few stars in the sky lit up her face. She was beautiful. Her hair reached down to the middle of her back. She wore Nina's pearl-colored linen vest with a thin piece of leather tied around the waist, holding it together over her bare chest. She looked like a hippie. She leaned through the car window and kissed her new boyfriend, Tom, on the lips. He handed her a can of beer, and she took a long pull on it, tilting her head back toward the streetlamp.

My mother stood behind me; I could hear her teeth grind. She was mad and had a right to be. She was divorced;

she had spent the last thirty-six-plus hours taking care of her grandchild. Mostly, she was concerned. Scared, too. She tapped a Camel from the soft pack, pressed it firmly between her lips, and lit it. This wasn't going to be good.

When Bunny walked in the back door, I could see she hadn't slept in days. Everything about her was just a bit messy. It took only a second for Nina to jump on her; it was like when professional wrestlers climb up on the top rope and jump down, knocking their opponents to the ground with a blow of their arm. Bunny fell quickly but not easily. She was ready to fight back. She was always ready for a fight.

They tumbled in from the back porch, through the kitchen, and into the living room. My mom wrapped her arms around Nina's waist and pulled her away. Her arms and legs were still flying toward Bunny, who was now out of reach. Bunny began to scream at her. I heard Kristina wake up in what used to be my bedroom. I ran to her and picked her up out of the crib. The electricity had gone out again in that room, so I held her in the dark, bounced her in my arms.

Bunny cut Nina to shreds. She was so smart that she could hurt you, and hurt you fast, with the things she said.

"You're such a fucking bitch," Nina cried into her hands. Then she screamed, "YOU'RE A FUCKING BITCH!"

I set Kristina on the bed and covered her ears with my hands. "You're making the baby cry!" I yelled. "Stop it."

I kept repeating those lines over and over until I only heard them crying. No more yelling and screaming. I put Kristina back to bed. When I entered the living room, Bunny was passed out cold on the couch. Nina was pulling her vest off of Bunny, like undressing a doll or dead body with her

arms bent back over her head. Nina inspected the vest and wept as she disappeared into her room.

Lisa was in the pear tree and I was in the apple tree when I told her about the fight through my walkie-talkie.

"She was calling her a fucking bitch. Bunny was drunk. Over."

"What did your mom do? Over."

"She pulled Nina away. I was trying to get Kristina to stop crying. Over."

"Did you? Over."

"I think so. I think it was because I was yelling to them that the baby was crying. It was sad. Over."

"Nina does have cool clothes. Over."

"Yeah, but Bunny is messy and gets things on them. That's why Nina doesn't like to share. Over."

"She does keep her things nice. She's always vacuuming the floor and polishing her boots. Over."

"Yeah, it's funny. Over."

"It's funny she vacuums naked. Over."

"I don't know why. Over."

From the back porch, my mom yelled, "Lanie! Lisa! Supper's ready."

"I love eating here! Over and out," Lisa said.

Everything was always homemade, always from scratch. Sometimes I liked what Lisa's mom made from the box better than our stuffed cabbages, sauerkraut, sausage, and medley of fresh garden vegetables. But dinner at our house was pretty special.

We both jumped from the trees, bare feet sinking into the grass. We raced to the house. We didn't mean to race, it just happened that way.

Inside, the Phi Kappa Regan sorority was back to normal. Bunny and Kristina were sitting at the round table on our back porch, Kristina propped up on a few editions of white and yellow pages. Bunny was chopping tomatoes and cucumbers into small pieces, and Kristina picked them up with her fingers and popped them into her mouth. She sucked the juice from each bite and made a sound like a little chirp before she swallowed.

Nina was in her robe, which was loosely tied together and exposing a long V of bare skin from her neck down to her belly button. On the island counter, a big skillet sat atop the propane burner we used whenever we were making fried zucchini or fried green tomatoes or mountains of pasta. Nina had prepared some of Mom's homemade spaghetti. When my mom made it, she kneaded the tough mixture of semolina and water together with just a touch of salt and then put it into the extruder. I liked to catch the spaghetti as it came out and drape it over the little racks to dry. I made every layer perfect so that they matched and looked like a beautiful spaghetti curtain.

Nina must have been thumbing through *Gourmet* magazine because for dinner that night, we had the best thing ever. She picked through five pounds of snow crab. She chopped garlic. She seasoned cream. She added the garlic to the skillet with a lot of butter, then added the cream and reduced it just a little. She cracked pepper into it and squeezed in fistfuls of sliced lemons. Then she added the crab and pasta. She

turned off the burner. It took two large wooden spoons in both hands for her to mix it. The long strands pulled up from the skillet and released the smell of the briny crab—almost fishy (a word I used to describe things I didn't like when I was little), but it was perfect. We could also smell the tart lemon. Lisa and I looked at each other with our jaws open, salivating. When Nina was done mixing, she grated mounds of fresh parmesan cheese over the top. Until that day, I had only ever known Kraft parmesan cheese, which came from a green container that was neatly placed in the side compartment of our refrigerator door.

Nina portioned us large bowls of pasta that we all took to the back porch. My mom, Lisa, Nina, Kelley, Bunny, Kristina, and I sat down together and ate as much as we could. It was like nothing was wrong, none of us were worried. It was just another summer day.

Summer went on as usual. Swimming, softball, more arguments between my sisters. Bunny started bringing her boyfriend, Tom, around. My mom had dropped a few pounds on her latest diet and was obsessively talking about her school options, all of which eventually rejected her. Her application to be a flight attendant was declined—she assumed because of her age and weight.

My dad started picking me up every so often; we'd drive out to Miller Beach, near where he was shacking up with some lady. He would later tell me, during one of our few arguments, that she hated kids and I should be grateful it didn't work out. At the time, though, she was introduced to

me as his friend from work. We didn't know—or at least I didn't know—he was cheating on my mom back then, but eventually my mom figured it out.

Aside from that, we had a good time riding around in his little pickup truck. He told me stories, like he always did. I could see every vivid description he gave of bustling Gary, Indiana, back when it had been on its way to becoming a true big city. He described it to me just as my mom had—the dime stores, movie theaters, butchers, larders. His boxing tournaments. The markets on Sundays where there were wooden crates full of fresh grapes from California for the "Slovaks to make wine." How he wooed my mother.

Mom would tell that part differently, how she couldn't stand living at home and wanted to get out. She would have taken anyone. I know that's bullshit. I still look through their wedding album like it's new to me, each time. She loved him, and she was happy loving him.

It was a Saturday in late August when Nina, Kelley, Bunny, Kristina, and I waited for him to come get us. We sat at the picnic table. We were all sweating. A few of Kristina's curls stuck to her forehead. Bunny reached across the table and combed her fingers through her daughter's hair. She pressed the last few of her Camels toward the opening of the pack, twisted it up, and put it in the breast pocket of her T-shirt.

"May I have one?" Nina asked.

Bunny rolled her eyes and gave her one. This would normally be the start of a fight, but Nina took the cigarette and lit it, staring Bunny straight in the eyes until she looked away.

I could hear April in the barn, a far distance away. My dad pulled up in the driveway.

He got out and stood with his hands in his pockets. He wore khakis and a polo, which was weird but not completely out of character. We said a few awkward hellos. Bunny got into the cab and Kristina sat on her lap. Nina, Kelley, and I climbed into the bed of the pickup. As we rode away, I saw my mom's silhouette in the kitchen window, looking on.

We went to the Lake County Fair because my dad said the Porter County Fair was for the hillbillies. About ten years before, my sisters' childhood friend had been raped by one of the carnies. I remember hearing this story and feeling that every time we went to the fair, we weren't very safe. The carnies catcalled and lured you toward the rides, the games. I felt uneasy giving in to them, double-checking for my dad's approval before I took the baseball from the tattooed hand of the wiry man and threw it at the bottles. Even with the little bit of fear, though, I was intrigued. It didn't stop me from the rides or the games.

The fairgrounds smelled like everything you did or could love if you grew up in the country. There was manure, animals, straw, rawhide, cedar, grass clippings, beer, funnel cake, buttered corn, fryer oil, fried cheese, cigarette smoke, cotton candy. Like smoke from a bonfire, the fair aromas got stuck in your clothes and your hair for days. I loved every second of it. Maybe it was my predisposition to the dark side, as it was dark, depending on how you looked at it. For all the bad rap the carnies got, I could see myself as one. I could have easily joined their club. Their whiskey breath, faded tattoos, rolled-up sleeves, cigarettes dangling from their lips. It was

mysterious, the idea of living everywhere and nowhere at once, setting up spectacles in small towns overnight. I was ten; my ambitions weren't high. I had also dreamt of working at Dairy Queen purely to be within constant reach of bacon cheeseburgers, fries, and chocolate-dipped chocolate ice cream cones.

After we did all the fun things and I had won Kristina the biggest stuffed Winnie the Pooh, we sat to eat. My favorite was the fried rice from Lee's Wok—the name was scrolled in an Asian-style font on a piece of cardboard over a tiny trailer. There was one wok and one fryer. Your options were egg rolls, chicken fried rice, and beef with broccoli. But I didn't stop there. I also got fried summer vegetables and grilled corn smothered in butter. I loaded up the table and we feasted.

My dad asked a lot of questions about my mom. Kristina and I sat across from each other at the end of the table. She had a cob of corn on a paper plate before her, and her head just reached over the top of the table. Without holding it or asking me to help her, she sank her teeth right into it. I took a picture, which my mom still has on her fridge, nearly twenty-eight years later.

My dad spoke in a whisper to my sisters. It looked serious, but I didn't pay any attention. I played with Kristina and I quietly ate my rice, knowing I'd have to wait one full year to get this again. I took in the moment because even though I thought our worlds might be falling apart, here we were, being a family.

A few months later, my mom and I were looking out the window, waiting for my dad to come get us. My mom had kind

of done herself up. She had put on lipstick and new red eye-glasses. Her hair was shiny and burgundy now. I was told to dress nice. I wasn't sure what was happening, and I don't know how much I thought about it, but I could feel a bit of hope. Like when you buy a scratch-off ticket from the gas station, feeling like you'll get a couple bucks—and then you do.

New Moon was on Route 30, a mammoth of a restaurant atop a hill not far from Burlington Coat Factory. There were heavy red double doors that opened into an atrium and a red carpet that people at that time would have described as "oriental." The walls were wood-paneled, and it was dark, despite all the open space. The dining room was lined with booths along the walls, and in the middle, there were large round tables with circles of glass in the center, which spun so that diners could share dim sum. They only served it on Sundays in the early '80s but then stopped. I guess dim sum never took hold in our part of Indiana, but I loved it.

My dad hated booths because of his hernia, but he agreed to sit in one because that's what my mom wanted. He was being shy and sweet. He let her walk in front of him, pick a side, and sit down first. This wasn't new to her—this was how he had behaved when he first wooed her—but it was new to me. There were no jokes today about my mom's zodiac sign being the boar or the pig. There was no teasing about what she should or should not order based on her weight. I asked my mom to order for me—shrimp with lobster sauce, a side of fried rice, and egg drop soup. I was still too shy to talk to waitresses.

My dad asked if I could give them some time alone. He told me to go sit in the atrium and look at the fish. There was

the obligatory goldfish aquarium. The goldfish were quite handsome. I watched them swim in and out of the rocks, bright pink coral, and wavering seagrasses. They came up to the glass to look at me and made perfect little O shapes with their mouths. I don't know how long I sat there.

"Lanie," my dad called, "come back, the food is here."

I hopped back into the booth on my mom's side. I am not sure if it was intentional that I favored her during this time, but I did. I think that's just how things like this go.

They were different. I could feel it. My dad was looking at her in a loving way, pleading-like, sort of, maybe even pathetic. It was a look I would find myself directing at my girlfriends years later after nights of heavy drinking, blackouts, cheating, fistfights—whatever the cause, I'd find myself with that same face.

My dad reached across the table and grabbed my mom's hand. Her wedding ring was back on. That I noticed right away.

He looked at me. I tried to avoid eye contact and stared down at the shrimp swimming in the thick, fragrant gravy.

He said, "Lanie," and cleared his throat.

I forced myself to look up but couldn't meet his eyes; I looked at the US Steel emblem on his windbreaker.

"Your mom and I are not going to get divorced. I'm going to move back in." Really, he hadn't ever moved out; he'd just taken a few suitcases filled with his work clothes and shoes.

"OK," I said. Maybe some other kid's parents would have pestered them for more emotion. But my parents never pressed me for things like that. They knew me, and they knew to let me just be.

I sat silently for the rest of my meal. My appetite hadn't subsided amid all the heightened emotions. I ate all the shrimp first, then practiced with my chopsticks. I picked out the fermented black beans one by one and squished them with my tongue against the roof of my mouth. My mom took the opportunity to inject into the conversation everything she wanted changed. The thing that stuck with me was that she wanted to move from our farmhouse. Maybe not today, not tomorrow—but now it was out there. She didn't want to wear waders while doing his laundry or take three hours on Saturdays to mow the lawn or tend the garden while he was out.

I ignored this like it was some sort of fiction, like it was just a bad dream and was never truly going to happen. Losing that house would cause me the same grief as losing a best friend. It would be my divorce, and I'd never be the same again.

Chapter 5
First Drinks

LATE SUMMER 1994. GETTY WAS AS BEAUTIFUL AS fifteen-year-olds come. We sat in the grass and watched from a couple doors down as he stepped onto his front porch and stretched. His arm rose up over his head and his T-shirt lifted, exposing his thin torso and the faint outline of his muscles. He was the boy every white couple in America dreamed of having: blonde curls, blue eyes, olive-toned skin. He was perfect.

It was Saturday morning and we were in our volleyball gear: kneepads, striped shorts, itchy polyester shirts. We'd just gotten back to my friend Melissa's house from our match with St. Mary's, a school that always beat us. Those girls must have been fed better milk than us; they were all at least six inches taller, full of growth hormones and bloat. High school volleyball would be much harder. Melissa would continue to do very well and later get a scholarship to play in college. For me, it would be my last year playing.

Over the next year or two, I'd drop out of other sports, one by one. A wall in my room was lined with mitts, baseball bats, balls from basketball, softball, volleyball, running shoes, spiked shoes, kneepads. After I quit, they collected dust; each time I looked at them, I was washed over with guilt. Eventually I stopped looking at that wall. It was like every other thing—the stuffed Ewok, Barbie house, Pee-wee Herman doll, Curious George. They were just a backdrop. I lived in two worlds at once, childhood and young adulthood. I wanted the latter but always missed the former.

Michael, Melissa's older brother, was washing his Ford Probe in the driveway. "Hotel California" blasted through his stereo. We didn't know how cool of a song it was until Michael told us. When Melissa became the first of us to drive, we got an Eagles tape and drove around listening to "Hotel California" and singing it at the top of our lungs.

Getty shielded the sun with his hand and looked in our direction, and—not knowing how beautiful he was— waved real big. "Hey!" he called.

Melissa was better at talking to boys. Since I had still only recently discovered I was a girl, I wasn't there yet. We walked over. They chatted for a bit and I felt a mix of jealousy, admiration, desire. I wanted to be like him and look like him, *and* be able to talk like her to him. I felt out of place because I couldn't do any of those things.

"I've got vodka in here," he said. He was holding a red plastic cup with what looked like a melted chunk of shaved ice in its center.

Within a millisecond, faster than I could even think, the words barreled out of me like a freight train: "I want vodka."

It was like I instinctively knew that vodka was the answer to this inner chatter.

I had seen adults do this plenty. I knew it did something, and I wanted to know what that felt like even though I knew it was dangerous. I had never had anything more than the Mogen David my dad gave me before bed when I had a cough. I had developed a really good way of faking hacking into my hand at night. I liked the Mogen David. It put me to sleep.

"My parents aren't home," he said, smiling, "so I blended this."

"Ooh, daiquiris," Melissa said.

When I went to fancy restaurants like Red Lobster, my family would let me get a virgin strawberry daiquiri, which was cloyingly sweet and tart and loaded with artificial flavors. I loved it like the Slushes at Dairy Queen or the epic 7-Eleven Coca-Cola–flavored Slurpees, which Bunny liked too.

I was ready for the real thing, though, vodka and all.

We followed him into his house and sat down at a small breakfast table in the dimly lit kitchen. Melissa did most of the talking, and while I liked Getty and hoped he would like me, I didn't stand a chance. I stayed quiet for the most part and bit my fingernails.

He threw ice into the blender and then added vodka from a big plastic jug. He might not have known what he was doing, but he smiled at us while he did it. Then I picked the tops from fresh strawberries and handed the berries to him. He added them with a smile and a little shuffle-like dance. Based on how the adults I knew had behaved while drinking, he didn't seem too drunk, but I wasn't sure. He handed us each a plastic cup.

Vodka was not good. The drink was tart, sweet, but I liked the real strawberries, and the alcohol was hot going down my throat.

"Here, try it with lemon," he said while pinching a wedge over the top of my cup.

I sipped. I was nervous. *What if I get drunk? What happens? What about my mom when she gets me?*

He invited us to his room. We all lay down on the bed. Remembering it now, I believe my head was toward the north and the west was to my side, at the edge of the bed near the window. This was the side of the bed I would have slept on if it was my bed. There were a few posters on the walls, a couple of model cars, a crossbow, and a gun I assumed was a BB gun, but which might have been a real rifle. Getty was in the middle, and Melissa was on the other side of him. We were way, way too young to be doing the things this could lead to. Like the sorts of things parents might have nightmares about.

Jesus, though, it wasn't really like that at all. As far as I know, Melissa and Getty weren't doing anything. I certainly wasn't. We talked and acted silly, like we were drunk, but weren't. I didn't say much for fear of saying the wrong thing because I really had no idea what boys wanted to hear girls say. And since I still didn't imagine myself a girl, most of the time I was super fucking awkward. But his leg was touching mine, and under the covers he rubbed his thumb against my wrist. I realize it's likely that the same thing was happening on Melissa's side, but for that small amount of time I believed it was our secret. *Could Getty really actually like me?*

No. Getty didn't like girls like me. He liked girls to like him, girls like me and all other girls, and the ones he liked

back were the ones who knew how to laugh at the right times, twist their finger in their hair, and bat their eyelashes. Some girls are born with that know-how, I thought, or maybe they have mothers who were born with it. But my mom didn't teach me those things or nurture me into knowing them. She was just who she was, and so was I.

Later, when my mom picked me up, I don't think there was even a lingering scent of alcohol on my breath. I didn't feel anything. I might have gotten a little sense of heat in the back of my throat, and it was enough for me to know I wanted more. I was too afraid.

I'd never become Getty's girlfriend. Melissa wouldn't, either. Once, while playing ditch and hiding between the bumpers of two cars, he put his hand on my leg, very casually, as if he had to because there was nowhere else for him to support himself. After that day, Getty smiled at me a lot, but he still talked more with all the other girls.

After we started high school, we didn't see Getty too much. There were so many other boys, though none really as cute. Some liked me. I occasionally liked one back, but mostly it was disappointing. Boys were confusing. It seemed like one day they liked you and then the next day they also liked your best friend.

Boys weren't my problem, though—it was the girls. I knew I was feeling things for girls that were way different from how I felt for the boys. While beautiful in their own right, boys were an obligation. Girls were different, they were complex and exciting. It seemed so much more complicated to accept myself as a female, though, while knowing I was also attracted to females. I was too old now to go

home after school and slip into the lives of my imaginary friends. I couldn't escape that way anymore.

But confusion about sexuality wasn't the only reason alcohol was so pleasing to me. I was certainly born with "the allergy," as we call it in AA. Once I drink, I cannot stop. Let me explain.

Melissa and I had two other close friends, Kathy and Michelle. Kathy was Irish Catholic and one of ten children in her family, or something close to that. Her father sold insurance, and her mother was a housewife. They had this big house, a colonial with a big porch and large pillars that rose up three stories. It was set at the back of a long, manicured gravel driveway. Her father took pride in mowing the lawn as if he were a blue-collar man, but he obviously wasn't. Ten kids, all in private school from elementary to college? Sometimes he had business doing whatever insurance people do and would take his wife and leave all the kids at home. The parties at this house were rightly called "The Schumann Parties." Every couple of years, the party duties were passed down to the next kid in line.

The first of these parties, when we were freshmen, only involved about five of Kathy's friends, and we were all a little afraid to drink, sort of like that day with Getty. The following year, as sophomores, our confidence had exploded. On the pool deck in Kathy's backyard, I sat in a circle among my friends playing a drinking game. We clapped our hands together, hit our knees, then snapped our fingers in a rhythm while saying, "What's the name of that fucking game called what the fuck?"

Then I said, "Slow fuck, slow fuck, wish I was a tight fuck."

Amanda (a brunette who was later one of my first very real crushes and a best friend for a time) sat to my right. It was her turn then to say, "Tight fuck, tight fuck, wish I was a hard fuck."

Melissa, next to her, said, "Hard fuck, hard fuck, wish I was a butt fuck."

Kathy, next to her, kept the momentum going. You get the picture. The more we chanted, the louder we became. But if you lost the rhythm on your turn, you were obligated to drink. While some of the others only drank because the rules said they had to, it didn't matter to me—I kept filling up my plastic cup.

When we stopped playing, we sat for a while in the circle and talked. We laughed. I felt dizzy and light-headed and really, *really* good. I can't describe it as anything but euphoric; the feeling and thought that I was becoming drunk was *arousing*. I kept thinking to myself, *Holy shit, holy shit*—it was almost like the feeling just before orgasm (I had no idea what an orgasm felt like at that age). The more I drank and let loose, the more I felt like I had something to offer the world.

What was even better about it was that everyone was laughing, not at me but with me. For a while, I was charming and funny. A few of the older girls, some very pretty girls, ones that I could never be friends with because they were too pretty, were laughing too. They'd occasionally fall into me with laughter and I thought, *This is how it's done, be funny*. Their having even a little crush on me didn't seem that far out of reach, and I carefully flirted with them. I found ways to flatter them harmlessly. It was just enough attention, I

thought—even if not from a boy—to make them feel really good about themselves. I was even complimented back. They told me I was funny or cute or, even better yet, that I was beautiful.

Mostly, the beer made me relaxed, which was new, like I zipped up my skin and was comfortable in it, maybe for the first time. *What the hell?* As I drank, I felt like I could be myself, act like how I felt, and it all seemed *normal.*

We were lying on our backs now. I was spinning. One of the football guys, Tim, who would go on to impregnate Lisa at the ripe age of seventeen and by the age of thirty, have, like, six or seven kids, had to carry me over his shoulder up the stairs. He threw me in a room and locked the door. Michelle took a post to watch me. She was kind, with long brown hair and big hazel eyes. It seemed she always took on the job of watching us. I'm not sure what I had been doing or saying at that point, or if I was just plain drunk, but they wanted me out of sight. I could only remember being told I shouldn't drink anymore. I didn't know what that meant. Wasn't the point to have as much as possible and blast off into space or to the other side of the moon?

I pounded the door with my fists and kicked it. Kathy came in and yelled at me to calm down and go to bed. She told Michelle to keep me quiet. *What the heck did I do? Why was I being punished?* These questions would come to me later, but in that moment, I didn't want to stop. I wanted to feel good, to talk to the girls, to be part of the party.

I tired myself and eventually fell onto the bed and cried myself to sleep. A few brief scenes came back to me. I was raising hell on the pool deck, dancing, screaming to the

music, not listening to people when they told me to calm down. I felt ashamed.

The next day when I woke up, I looked in the mirror and I looked different. My face was bigger, probably from all the crying, but I could also see pores in my face. It was the strangest thing. I didn't feel good. I had never known a headache or thirst like that in my life, and I was happy I hadn't thrown up in my sleep, as I knew my sisters had before. It occurred to me as I stood in the bathroom with my face under the faucet, gulping water, that I felt like I was Bunny. My body was like hers, my movements felt like hers. If Bunny was an alcoholic, then I was too. I owned it and was ready to take it on. I had a new identity.

A year or so later. "I like the way your sparkling earrings lay, against your skin so brown." I was singing.

Kate laughed, then joined in. "And I wanna sleep with you in the desert tonight, with a billion stars all around."

Deep River was magic. The oak trees were tall and old, and you could smell the decayed leaves on the ground thawing from the winter. I hunted mushrooms there with my dad when I was a kid. Kate and I were lying on the picnic table. We looked up at the blue sky floating above the trees. It was about seventy degrees, one of the first nice days of the year.

Chloe danced over, holding a Mickey's malt liquor. She wore bells on her shoes, a colorful long skirt, and a tank top. She sang, "I got a peaceful, easy feelin'."

Kate looked like a Mexican Irish beauty queen. Her skin was really brown, and her sparkling earrings were made of

silver, turquoise, and feathers. A crocheted hemp necklace with a tiny amber bead in its center rested against her clavicle.

I opened another Mickey's and tried to make out the puzzle on the inside, but I couldn't. I was feeling pretty good. Earlier that day in the cafeteria, Craig, Kate's boyfriend, who was a fucking asshole, walked past me while grabbing his crotch. The implication was, *Suck it.*

Kate saw me get pissed. "Ignore him," she said.

He and Kate were fighting, so his revenge was to patronize anyone close to her. I'd known Kate since kindergarten. Craig was a jealous guy and sometimes threw her around. I could never figure out why she put up with him. He had bad skin and a scrunched-up face, like a human pug dog, and coarse, dishwater-blonde hair.

Guys like him—all I could see was red. Explosive blood red. I would have liked to take his dick, twist it off, and shove it down his own throat. I think the thought might even have excited me. *All hail, Aileen Wuornos.* I put my fists on the table and stood up. I took my bowl of taco salad—something I loved very much, but this was going to be worth it—and walked over to Craig, who sat laughing with some of his friends, all jerks. I dumped it over his head. I pushed the red and white checkered boat until I could feel the tortillas crunching against his skull. Once he realized what was happening, a flurry of expletives flew at me from all the boys at the table. I turned around and ran. Craig got up to chase me but was stopped by a teacher.

That afternoon Kate and Chloe stopped me outside the bathroom, where I had just been smoking. I'd go into the stall, take two drags, snuff it out, then zip it back in my book

bag. Carrying around a little ashtray, I smelled horrible. How I thought I wouldn't get caught was beyond me, but I didn't. I didn't need the nicotine. I only did it because it was against the rules, and that gave me a little rush.

Kate laughed when she smelled me. "You're ridiculous," she said.

"You're a badass," Chloe exclaimed.

"Want to go to Deep River after school? I've got twelve Mickey's."

"Somehow that seems like too many and not enough for the three of us," I replied. "I can't. I have softball practice."

They rolled their eyes.

After school, the team changed in the locker room, and I really stayed away from everyone. I wasn't in the mood for talking or laughing or trying to fit in. Lisa would have been my only friend on the team by then, but we really weren't friends anymore. Nothing happened that ended our friendship; it was just that I became more of a deviant than she did. I mean, she smoked and drank sometimes, but she just wasn't as bad as I was. I can't even think back to who her friends were, but by then I had a different crowd. She sat at one end of the team, and I at the other. I smiled and waved. She waved back.

I wasn't good at softball anymore. The girls pitched too fast in high school, and I never caught up. They had me as a pitcher for a bit, but I couldn't throw it that hard. A girl who had been at St. Mary's was the better pitcher. (The milk, you know.) I didn't practice, as I was now more interested in other things.

Our coach was talking, and I could not hear him. I. Just. Couldn't. Do men anymore today. Behind me, in the school

parking lot, I could see Chloe and Kate smoking a cigarette. They stood beside Kate's VW Jetta. They waved when they saw me look.

Before I knew it, the coach was talking at me. Yelling at me, actually, to pay attention. When I focused again, I heard him say, "Sweetheart." That *sweetheart* sounded like a fucking ice scraper on the windshield in zero-degree weather. To this day, I still feel bad for throwing my mitt and bat and calling him "a child-molesting piece of shit" right in front of his daughter, who was one of my teammates. He wasn't, as far as I know.

I left and never went back, for various reasons, obviously.

There I was, in white T-shirt, softball pants—tight from my waist to my calves—cleats, ball cap, ponytail. In Kate's car, I dug through my book bag and handed her a new tape I'd bought at Hegewisch Records. Jefferson Airplane. We went to the park. "White Rabbit" and the warm spring air whispered over my skin. Chloe told me to grab a Mickey's from under her seat. I did. The hairs on my arms stood up like antennas. If you know anything about how alcohol works on people like me, with the allergy, then you know that once I opened it and took that first drink, everything was right with the world again. We were going to Deep River. We'd drink, get buzzed, dance. We'd smoke cigarettes.

"Hey," I said. "Want me to show you how to find mushrooms?"

"To get high?" they asked, in unison.

"No, for sustenance. To eat." My passion was clear. They said I was weird. Didn't matter—once I was through with my first Mickey's, I didn't care.

Chapter 6
Goodbye

THE AUCTIONEER LOOKED JUST LIKE A PIG, REALLY, like a lot of auctioneers you might imagine. Bib overalls, white cotton shirt, straw hat, fat belly, buttons about to pop, steel-tip cowboy boots, red face. My dad ran frantically around our yard, through the house, grabbing things out of the auctioneer's chubby fingers, standing in protest before his tractor, arms splayed like an eagle's wings, saying, "This isn't for sale," or "No, not this either." You could see people roll their eyes, huff and puff, some leaving, because *was it for sale or was it not?*

My mom watched from the back porch, feeling divine retribution, while the world my dad loved crumbled. She had wanted the house gone for a long time now. She was working at Carson's in the mall, now using him since he had begged for mercy. We were moving to a subdivision, a *really* terrible one. She got a town house, without a yard to maintain or a

garden for him to work in, and with a real washer and dryer. Dad was about to get busier at work. He'd have less to come home to since my mom had stopped needing him in the same way and now had more friends and a paycheck.

I'd just get jolted.

Nina and I ended up sharing a bedroom. Her mattress was on the floor, always tidy. I had a daybed in the corner and my own tiny dresser. I still wasn't allowed to touch her things, but sometimes I slept in her bed when she wasn't home, on top of the comforter so as not to mess up anything. I'd run my hands over the top in the morning, straightening it as best I could. Still very careful about the carpet, I treaded lightly.

I could never have imagined leaving the farmhouse. I felt bad for myself but even worse for my dad. Maybe this was just how he showed his love—working hard, being gone, tending a garden to feed his family. My mom didn't speak that language, though. It was like they were trying to say the same thing, but one spoke Russian and the other spoke German. It just was one big misunderstanding.

The farmhouse was where I had all my best memories. The best feelings, like waking up Christmas morning and finding a bike on the roof or walking along the barn fence, pretending it was a tightrope. I danced on that fence when *Dirty Dancing* came out. I was a very good Patrick Swayze.

The sun was almost as hot as the time I got heatstroke. My dad looked on the verge of cardiac arrest. The auction was raging. People kept coming and going. I walked through the yard to our apple tree. I stepped on something hard and lifted my bare foot to inspect: it was a green plastic army man.

It was the one that crawled along the ground with his gun at his side. I felt like that now, down low as I could be, hoping all of it would go away. That it was just some fake thing that was happening, and we wouldn't really end up moving. I put the army man in the pocket of my jean shorts and climbed the tree. I sat on my favorite branch. It was formed like the shape of a picnic table. I folded my arms over the branch before me and rested my chin on my hands. Nothing smelled or tasted better than those apples in the early fall. I decided right at that moment that someday I would buy the place back. I didn't want to go. That place was me. That place was also my dad. That place was everyone and everything I loved. It was even my mom, though she wouldn't admit it.

That day we sold the farmhouse and all of its contents at auction. My dad sat in the empty barn with his head hung. A carcass of himself, like all the animals he'd emptied before. Sometimes, even now, he'll recall the things he had and say, "Your mother got rid of it when we sold the farmhouse."

I got terribly sunburnt that day, but I didn't care. I wanted to hurt. Pain was manageable. I was trying to figure out how to match my outsides with my insides. The truth is, life felt more secure and more alive the summer my parents were split up. The day felt like the beginning of some sort of end, and it was.

The summer before, Bunny and Kristina had moved out. That was hell. They moved to Georgia with Bunny's boyfriend, Tom. No one thought it was a good idea. Tom was the kind of guy who looked at my other sisters' butts and said

things like, "Packin' on the pounds, huh?" I imagined punching him in the face. A lot. I didn't weigh much more than a wet rag, and if he ever said anything to me, it was about my surfboard-shaped body—long, narrow, without much curve, "a human stick figure."

Bunny had been listening to John Prine in her room while she packed. She sang along, something about moving to the country, throwing out the TV, and so on. She threw her clothes into boxes as she bounced from dresser to closet and Kristina mimicked her, occasionally picking up a bra that had been flung across the bedpost or a pair of panties from the floor, or taking one of her "princess" dresses from a hanger.

I hated this. I asked Bunny about the song.

She said with her best southern accent, "Yeah, we're gonna be in the real country."

She lifted a can of Budweiser to her lips and looked at me over the top of the can. It was OK when she did things like this, drink beer in the morning. Her eyes were big and green and gray. Her hair was long, blonde, a little dirty and messy. Her skin was lightly tanned. She was beautiful and therefore, I figured, she could do whatever she wanted. It was just how the world worked, I thought. *The real country?* But we *are* in the country, I wanted to say, but I didn't. I sat on the bed and nervously bounced my legs.

"Hey, look," she said. "You don't have to be worried."

"I'm not," I said.

"We'll be back in a couple months to pick you up." She sat next to me with a book in her hand. "And then we will go to the Dead show in Indy and drive back down to Georgia. You'll stay a couple weeks."

"What's that?" I asked, tilting my head at the book.

"*Jitterbug Perfume*." She handed it to me. "Read it and we'll talk about it when I come to get you."

"OK."

I looked at Kristina. The sun was coming in just perfect over her curls, which in the summer were so much lighter. I loved her so much, but I was worried. I had seen Tom spank her a couple times, and it made me hate him more. Once, I rode in the back seat of his little tan Mustang convertible while we'd driven out to the lake and had dinner at The Hacienda, where my sister swore by the chile rellenos. I had been feeling good earlier that day. Tom was smart and fun and charming sometimes, and it was my hope in those moments that he was going to stay this way, instead of how he was at other times—a pretentious prick. I was having fun and feeling love for everyone. I lifted my face to the dark sky. The moon flew past faster than ever as he accelerated up the tree-lined street. The Rolling Stones sang, "Goodbye Ruby Tuesday," and Kristina, tiny as ever and smarter than any other kid, *obviously*, sang along with Mick Jagger. It delighted my sister. That night was nothing short of my wildest dreams.

But then suddenly it was late, and Kristina got cranky and she started to whine. Tom swung the car to the highway shoulder, coming to a stop so fast the gravel popped up and tinged against the bottom of the car. The crickets were loud. He put his hand on the back of my sister's headrest and turned around.

He said, looking like a snaggletoothed bogeyman, "Shut up, goddamn it."

I thought, *What the fuck?* Then he reached over and spanked her legs with a swift little pop of the wrist. I wanted to bite his face. I wanted to do whatever I could that would hurt him as much as possible. Kristina looked scared but didn't really stop crying. My sister didn't do anything, just kept looking forward, not even at him. I thought surely she would tell him not to touch her daughter. But she didn't. When he began to drive again, I scooted next to Kristina and put my arm around her. I put my other hand across her lap as if I could take away the sting from the spanking.

I told my mom about this as soon as I got her alone that night. She sat on the edge of my bed as I lay there, too upset to sleep, and recounted the details. The rage swelled inside of me until I started to cry and couldn't stop. I hadn't cried in some time, so I just began to cry about everything that had happened over the past several months. I felt a release. It hurt just as much as it felt good.

The day they moved out, some part of my life closed shut. Like whatever my life could have been if they had stayed was now out of my reach. I don't know what that might have been—just some sort of parallel dimension. My parents were back together, but my sister and niece were leaving. I suppose I wanted nothing more than to keep all of us together. It felt safer that way, all of us under the same roof. The noise all of us made was the pulse. There was an excitement in the arguments, the making up, the large meals, the chaos, the clutter. It's what made the farmhouse our home.

I felt the same way, maybe even worse, the day we moved our things out of the farmhouse. I don't remember packing—perhaps I had refused to. I just remember shuffling

my feet through the gravel. I remembered the last time I had prayed for the mother ship to come take me away. For a long while, I had stood there, bare-chested, socks in my shorts, with a haircut like the top of a mushroom around my head. *God, if you're up there*, I had asked him, *make me a boy. Turn me into a boy, God. Something is not right here. I want to do the things they do. I want to be powerful too.* When we left the farmhouse, I left that boy there too. I knew there was nowhere else I could be him.

Part Two

Chapter 7
Interlude—Girls

1984. I FELL IN LOVE WITH BOY GEORGE. I SAT ON THE living room floor and ate a hard-boiled egg with a little salt and pepper. That was my afternoon snack. Sometimes I'd eat two or three. Boy George was on the television. He was pretty. I liked watching him. I'd never seen anyone like that before. He was a man and a woman, and it was amazing.

My dad came in the room and stood behind me. He chuckled. "Sissy," he said. "Faggot," he reinforced.

I was five but I knew he was trying to say something and that it was supposed to influence me. Like any good rebel, I only became more interested. What a sham.

Annie Lennox was another one. A beautiful woman in a suit. I couldn't take my eyes away. Watching her on the television was like how people think they get healed through the palms of their preacher. At the vision of Annie Lennox in that suit, talking about the rain coming again, I was

all zonked, in some sort of trance. I'd be in the yard, alone, singing it through a stick microphone. Dancing in my little shorts. I could be Annie Lennox someday. And Boy George.

1995. Rick turned the volume up. Beastie Boys. We shouted in unison, "GIRLS, ALL I REALLY WANT IS GIRLS AND IN THE MORNING IT'S GIRLS."

We faded out so we could carefully pass the roach. A heavy cloud drifted from Rick's lips and nostrils out the window as he yelled, "JOCKING MIKE D TO MY DISMAY."

Rick's Pontiac was a hand-me-down from his dad. The seats were lumpy, and above our heads the cloth from the ceiling formed stalactites and bubbles. There was a box of old car stereos and other electronics from the last decade that Rick was set on fixing.

Rick might have liked me at one point. That's sort of how it was with boys and girls, but it always seemed easier to be friends with boys. I knew how they felt, and I could also tell them the inner workings of a girl's mind, sometimes. Whenever I thought Rick's affections might have turned toward me, I flipped it toward my friends. "Melissa's cute," I said, or "I think my cousin Mandy likes you." I told him I could mention something to them. This worked. I sort of became the unofficial liaison, not just for Rick but for most of the boys.

We thrusted along Randolph Street, our stomachs floating up and down as Rick accelerated over the hills. We passed Mr. Elich's farm. With the windows down, I could smell that part of childhood. The trees and brambles zipped by my periphery, along with the spots where I'd later crash

cars, get poison ivy while running from the police, and eventually forage cattail pollen, milkweed flowers, and elderberries. Smells like that were the pure essence of outdoors. In the spring, the lilacs were my favorite. At sixteen, talking to my friends while we walked along a ditch somewhere, I'd pick a berry and recall scent memories; the smell of lilacs reminded me of the farmhouse, and wild black raspberries of my grandfather's farm. My friends told me I was an old soul for reminiscing in this sort of way, although they didn't say it like that. To them, I was mysterious and weird.

We drove down Old Lincolnway and past the farmhouse. I didn't live there anymore, and my heart was still broken. Now I shared a room with Nina in a townhome, and she wasn't home that much. We went past the train tracks, headed for Melissa's. Rick liked her. Lisa's house was on the left. Lisa was my first best friend and first crush. Our friendship didn't start in the conventional way—building with blocks together in preschool or playing with a dollhouse or sharing glue, all of which we eventually did. It started because I, "the mute," decided to write a love letter.

1983. Every night I took a bath, and every night I had the same question. "When is school over?"

"You just started," my mom replied.

Each morning, I asked her to pick me up early from school. I only felt safe and happy when we had line-up at the end, and I could see her face through my classroom door.

Once, I forgot to ask her to pick me up, and as she left, I realized what I had done. I fell to the classroom floor in

hysterics. The little girl who never spoke, never looked you in the eye, suddenly screamed as if someone were stabbing her with pencils. Tears streaked my face as I hyperventilated and the other children ran to form a circle around me and watch. Mrs. Boyle picked me up from the floor and cradled me in her arms. The children from the next classroom over formed the outer circle. It was not just a fuss but a full-on spectacle. Darlene Camacho petted my head, shushed me, and whispered it would be OK.

When they could finally get me to calm down enough to say what was wrong, I spat out, gasping for air, "I. Forgot. To. Tell. Her. To. Come. To. Get. Me. Early."

Mrs. Boyle and the other kids tried to reassure me that my mom would be back for me. I was uncertain.

My mom never forgot to pick me up. Never. She was never even late.

I remember her standing before me at the start of one school day. Her face was tender, and I looked down at the buttons of her jacket. She wore a yellow vinyl raincoat with snap buttons. I began to snap and unsnap them. I was wasting time. "I'll be back to get you," she said.

"I know," I whispered, "but early?" I turned back to look at the classroom. There were things there to do, kids to play with, a dollhouse that I very much wanted to explore, but there were always some other kids playing with it and I couldn't get myself to join them.

When the bell rang, all of the kids packed up their pencil boxes and began to file behind one another. They laughed and pushed. I stayed behind, packing my things with purpose: each pencil facing the same way, the erasers from big

to small, the crayons from darkest color to lightest. I put my pencil case beneath my arm and stood at the end of the line. I didn't want to look toward the door. I was afraid my mom wouldn't be there, but I did look. Her face was pressed against the glass. She smiled and waved at me. That's all I needed—my mom and returning home.

A girl a little taller than me, with olive skin and long brown hair, turned around and kindly smiled in my direction. I looked to see if there was someone behind me and there wasn't. She was smiling at me. That was Lisa.

On the way to the Bronco parked at the end of the block, I told my mom about the girl.

"Oh," she said, "we can invite her over to swim."

That sounded nice. I wasn't sure how it would work, though. Would I actually have to talk to her? I asked my mom to ask Lisa's mom.

She lifted me onto the passenger seat and asked, "Did you go potty in your pants today?"

"No, I didn't have to go."

Going to the bathroom in my pants was a thing. When she picked me up, my mom always brought a bath towel from home, folded neatly over the passenger seat. In her purse, she'd have a pair of shorts or jeans and clean underwear for me to change into if I'd had an accident. They weren't accidents. The only time I had been brave enough to use the bathroom alone, two boys had walked in and pointed, laughing. This closed my mind to all future trips. Plus I feared I'd get locked in somehow. Instead, I sat on the floor behind the dollhouse and between the bookshelves and peed my pants. I had decided it was safer.

That evening, I used Elizabeth's sketch pad and charcoals to draw Lisa a picture. I needed a way to communicate how I felt. There was a rainbow, heart, and lion. It read in a careful but clumsy scrawl, "To Lisa," then at the bottom, "Love Iliana."

To be clear, this was every bit as much a love letter as it was an invitation to be my friend. This was my first time trying to make a friend who wasn't already built in as family. Since I didn't understand how to talk with the other children, an expression of my deepest feelings through a paper medium was the best I could do.

Lisa wore sundresses. Her hair was thick. She smiled at me as I walked up to her desk. I took the folded piece of paper from my pencil box and placed it in front of her. I scurried back to my seat and put my head down with my arms folded around it. I felt like I might have put my heart on her desk. It was a strange feeling. The difference between the two of us was obvious. She was a regular child who could talk to adults and kids, smile, respond to what it was the teacher asked when called upon. I, on the other hand, heard the teachers as though they spoke another language. They had to show me everything, step by step. I couldn't talk to the other kids. I didn't understand smiling was to show kindness.

She read my letter. A few minutes later, she was in front of me. It might have been my alien powers that allowed me to sense her standing before me. I slowly looked up and she smiled, sympathetically. Somehow, I already understood she couldn't be my girlfriend, but she could be my friend—at least, I hoped.

I tried to think of every way I could to stop going to

school. I felt like I simply couldn't do it. But knowing that I was going to have a friend made it a little better. During recess, Lisa invited me to sit with her and her friends. I did but didn't talk to them. I was teased for peeing my pants, and sometimes I got dirty looks. But Lisa just smiled kindly and continued to include me. I wasn't like these girls in any shape or form. Lisa was more like them, but she was gentle. Lisa allowed me to feel normal even though I didn't feel like it.

Eventually, Lisa became my best friend and showed me how to be a girl.

1997. I was eighteen. As my friends packed up their L.L.Bean duffels and bounced happily out of their houses in Gap summer dresses and Banana Republic shorts and shirts, waving and kissing goodbye to childhood, I sat at the desk in my room and did lines of coke off my pile of college rejection letters. It wasn't that I was incapable of getting good grades; it's just that I was already a full-blown alcoholic. True, I wasn't as book smart as my peers. I had something else. I felt it, but I couldn't name it.

I smoked a cigarette out the window of my room as dusk settled in, and then Chloe showed up outside, down below. Chloe was my new Lisa, but different. We met when I was a sophomore and she was a freshman. Her locker and my cousin Mandy's locker were next to one another. Chloe had long brown hair and probably the biggest green eyes I'd ever seen. She was not pretty in a conventional way, but with all that hair, and those eyes with their spider-leg lashes, and that smile, she was very alluring.

That allure was mostly the reason why most of the other girls didn't like her. I sort of didn't like her either but not because of the allure. I just thought she was stupid. She talked like a Valley girl, using lots of "likes," "totallys," "rads," and words like that. She wasn't from the West Coast. Regardless, she had become my friend, slowly, through association. When I started driving, she ended up in my car pool because she lived down the road. Groggy mornings turned into stoned mornings, or mornings playing the music so loud our ears burst, or laughing, or stressing out each time I came to a stop and had to put the 1984 Crown Victoria in neutral in order to keep it from dying.

I guess Chloe was sort of a slut—maybe that's why it wasn't so unusual that she was one day "gay" and my girlfriend. I don't know how it happened. Maybe it was one too many drinks too many times that started the curiosity, the crush, the flirting. I didn't think I carried myself as someone who might be gay, although I wasn't shy about letting my friends know about the crushes I had on woman movie stars; that seemed safe to say. Anyone could admire the beauty of an on-screen actress. This particular summer, after I had graduated, we had lots of crazy nights. One night was very distinct from the others. We had what remained of a half gallon of Captain Morgan rum, a spirit we cherished. We'd had the bottle for a couple days, though it wasn't unusual for us to polish one off in a night.

I had on my "bikini"—a little pair of cutoff jeans and a tank top—and my hair up in a bun. The night was perfect, as summer nights go in Indiana. As we walked to the community pool, I looked up at the sky and could see both the Big and Little Dippers.

It was the late '90s, but we had a group of friends who followed the Dead; we listened to classic rock, wore hippie skirts and tie-dye, went camping, and snacked on things in the wild. We were neo-hippies. We were caught between childhood and what it all really meant; we still lived in our parents' houses, the threat of adulthood lingered, and college loomed.

We climbed the gate. I sent the half gallon of rum over first. Before I could get comfortable, Chloe stripped off her clothes and told me to take off mine too. She stood naked, her perfect breasts framed by her long brown hair. Her torso was long and flat, with a bit of definition, even, which I've always thought was very pretty on women. I've had a little potbelly since I was a baby. A triangle of fluffy hair covered her between her legs; I was surprised to see it was trimmed and quickly averted my eyes. I had never even thought of grooming the hair between my legs. At this point, I still had not had sex, seen porn, or even really thought about doing those things. I didn't know what an orgasm was, let alone how to achieve one. I wouldn't learn about that until I was twenty-four, when reading erotica would help me figure that out. (Sorry to everyone I had "sex" with before then.)

I looked her in the eyes. I could feel my face flush. Her eyelashes fluttered. I did not take my clothes off. I was too shy, at least without the alcohol in me. At the sight of Chloe's trimmed hair, I realized I needed tiny scissors too.

"OK." She shrugged and jumped in. I jumped in behind her.

Nothing really happened that night. I was chivalrous and walked her home. Maybe it was because I was older.

Maybe it was because I thought Chloe needed protection, from herself. We were comfortably buzzed. We talked about drinking more, but we didn't have anything. I thought a long walk home and a cigarette would at least settle me down from the itch to really tie it on. I always got that itch. Soon as I could feel that little bit of heat go down my throat, my body would get all warm and start to tingle. I'd suddenly feel so much better. I didn't want that feeling to end.

"I'll see you tomorrow," I said.

She leaned forward and kissed me on the lips. Long enough to make it more than friendly. There was no tongue. No movement. No touching. Just a clip of time that made it something it wasn't before. Young, inexperienced, more than curious about my lifelong attraction to women, I was sold. Back then, a kiss was all I needed to become devoted.

1986. On Halloween day, Melissa wore spangled bracelets, lots of makeup, and an off-the-shoulder, netted T-shirt. I wore my homemade pirate costume: shredded jeans, a striped shirt, a red handkerchief around my head. I had a plastic sword, and from electrical tape I'd cut out a nice mustache that I'd stuck above my lip. I was feeling myself, you know? Like when you feel as if you look *really* good. Being able to dress up like a pirate with a mustache made me feel more like myself than I did on any regular day. It's my dad's fault, really. He'd make mustaches for me from electrical tape, put a large dull kitchen knife in my hand, and declare a sword fight. When he asked me what we were fighting for, I'd declare, "The princess," while pointing at

my sister Nina, sitting cross-legged on the shag rug of our living room floor.

I pulled the same move with Melissa as I had with Lisa in preschool: a very carefully constructed note, this time in the medium of chalk and sketch paper, depicting a heart with rainbows and unicorns. I dropped the lion bit. Even though I had made Lisa into only a friend with that note, I still thought I could woo girls. By the end of the day, I had gained enough courage to give her my letter. Melissa wasn't as kind as Lisa; she looked at the letter and then showed it to her friends, who were also dressed as Madonna. They looked at me and laughed.

I'm not sure at the time any one of us would have known the terms *homosexual, gay,* or *lesbian,* but one of the girls said simply, "You're not a boy."

It felt like she had taken my sword and thrust it through my stomach up to my throat. I looked down and fumbled with my hands. "It's from Ryan," I said without hesitation, slightly surprised I could lie so on point.

Ryan was sort of a friend because my mom and his mom had Tupperware parties together. While they displayed Tupperware and ate potato salad, we played with He-Man in his room and talked about how he wanted Melissa to be his girlfriend.

Ryan immediately said, "It's not from me."

I lied right in front of him, *about* him, as if he were delusional: "Yeah, you told me to write it to her."

"No, I didn't."

I was mortified. "He did." By now I had to believe it myself. I really wanted to disappear.

They continued to laugh, and I knew I couldn't figure my way out of this. I went back to my desk, put my head down into my crossed arms, and swallowed the boulders rolling up into my throat.

1996. The Schumann Party. Like every good John Hughes movie. Kegs. Streamers. Football players. Pom-pom girls. The cool kids. The nerdy kids. The goth kids. The druggies. Everyone came, whether they were invited or not. Melissa and I had gone to grade school with Kathy, and we were all friends. Rick was there. Melissa's brother had supplied us with the kegs. The parties at the Schumann house were historic. Now, with Kathy's siblings in college, the party was left to us.

Melissa liked Andy. Kathy liked Andy too. Amanda liked John. I had a boyfriend from another school, but I didn't talk to him much. His name was Ben and he was very cute, but Karen, who we really didn't like and who had boobs bigger than all of us, flirted with him all the time. It didn't leave me any real chance. He secretly liked her. Weird being teenagers, you know—like, *Why didn't Ben just date Karen instead? Why did he stay with me? Why'd I even date a boy in the first place?*

I told Melissa the deal in history class. We both had a crush on Mr. Gothe, with his wild gray hair, goatee, and John Lennon glasses. But my crush was more like admiration or something. His classroom smelled like old books and formaldehyde; the previous year, it was where we'd learned to identify a frog's intestines, heart, and liver. We didn't have air conditioning, so smells like that never went away. The

humidity pushed them further and further into every pore. I slid Melissa a note tucked under my penny loafer. She sat behind me. She had asked if Ben was coming to Kathy's over the weekend. I said I hadn't talked to him in over a week. And that she knew how I felt about him anyway.

Let's pause here really quick. Melissa, who is, at the time of this writing, still a very good friend to whom I still send a text every year on her birthday, is the same Melissa who laughed at me when I gave her that love letter. OK.

The note read, "You know how I feel about boys. It seems necessary to like them, but I sort of don't. They like me so it's easy. I'm more interested in hippie girls, pom-pom girls, smart girls, any girls really are better than boys."

Melissa would laugh at me when we'd go to concerts and we'd get tipsy. She'd flirt with boys and I'd flirt with girls, and it wasn't that weird. It was easy and it sort of worked.

I did mess around with Ben a couple times. We didn't have sex. I didn't have sex until it accidentally happened with everyone's grade-school crush shortly after high school. It was terrible and it hurt. I was high on coke and rum; it was never going to happen with a guy because I loved him, so I might as well figure out what fucking was all about, I thought. My crotch hurt for two days afterward, and I got a yeast infection. He was the kind of guy who, if I looked him up today, and I haven't, would turn out to be fucking bloated as a toad.

At Kathy's, we sat on the front porch and drank Miller High Life from red Solo cups. I felt confident and sexy. I could even stand up straight and genuinely smile while holding eye contact. Until I began to see two of everything. I had

on green Nike tennis shoes and a bandana around my head, sort of like Axl Rose. That's what Jennifer said—that I looked like Axl Rose. Sure, he was hot, in a girly sort of way ... and if she thought I looked like him, then maybe she was attracted to me in that way? I didn't look like a guy, though. I never have. Maybe it was my energy, because the girls sometimes flirted with me. They did. It was subtle, but I think Jennifer sort of liked me. She voted for me for best-looking in our senior class, and for best smile. I saw when I looked at her ballot in algebra class.

When Jennifer showed up, she was alone. She had brown hair that was a little red, too, in the light. Every time you thought maybe you'd find an inconsistency or something boring, you couldn't. Her lips were full and she wore a sort of red purplish lipstick. Her eyelashes were thick. She didn't look like anyone else; you couldn't say, "Oh, you look like so-and-so." It just wasn't there. She was a little shorter than me. She wore a Cubs jersey that was a little loose. The shorts she wore were quite tiny, and of course I noticed her butt, though I would have never thought to comment on it. Or even think of it for too long. The boys said to one another under their breath, "Hey look," in reference to its apple shape. I watched them look at her, and it made me mad. If I had a crush on someone, I surely didn't tell anyone. I *really* had a crush on her. Melissa might sometimes know if there was a girl at the receiving end, but I was afraid of scaring people. I didn't want my friends to worry I might like them in a way I didn't. I did like Jennifer, but no one knew except us.

I flirted with her, gently. Little comments about how it

wouldn't be possible for her not to get any boy she wanted. Or, "Whatever, you have the most beautiful smile." They were comments that weren't necessarily out of the ordinary for girls who are friends to say to one another. For us, though, sometimes it felt different—at least to me. She'd get mad at me if I forgot to greet her when we saw each other out. It's not that I forgot; sometimes I didn't say hi only because I was nervous.

Once, in the car on the way home, I asked her why she wasn't talking to me. She said, "You hurt my feelings."

I asked, "Why?"

"Because you didn't say hi. You just ignored me like I wasn't there."

"I'm sorry," I said, and then when I got out of the car, we embraced in my driveway, all in darkness, no streetlights, while the birds started to chirrup, and she kissed me on the cheek. My heart dropped. I went inside, up to my room, under my covers, and smiled until I fell asleep. I swore to myself that next time, I'd kiss her back but on the lips, just very fast. I liked her from freshman year until we graduated.

Oh, girls. I might have even loved some of them, like Jennifer. But I wasn't sure I liked girls the way the boys liked girls. They talked about boobs and butts, drooled about them. I wanted to strangle them for talking like that. I wanted to protect girls from them. I thought the prettiest parts of women's bodies were their eyes, or smile, or gestures. Like when a girl touched my arm while laughing at something I said or stacked her books neatly in a pile before putting them in her book bag. Or how she ate a peanut butter and jelly sandwich with the crust cut off.

Or how, when Jennifer asked me to light her cigarette, I fumbled with my crumpled matchbook and she took it out of my hand and lit two, one for me and one for her.

"You shouldn't use matches," she said.

We sat on Kathy's front porch. I formed my lips into an O and blew smoke rings, and she blew smoke rings into my smoke rings. I swore to myself I was going to kiss her. If I hadn't turned around and seen everyone else on the porch, we could have been completely alone. Just us and the cicadas.

I never kissed her.

Chapter 8
First Jobs

HIGH SCHOOL SUCKED A SMALL FLACCID DICK. I'LL SKIP over most of it.

The first year, I was mocked terribly, but as I slowly came out of my delusions and conformed more to how the other girls behaved and acted, I blended in.

I crashed a couple cars. I ended up in jail twice. I excelled at chemistry and mathematics and thought I'd go to school for engineering someday, but I wasn't accepted into any of the colleges I applied to. My parents wouldn't let me go away to college anyway.

I hated high school. It was like prison, in a way. I could have been at either. I graduated in 1997, somehow, but I thought I might die first.

People like Jill, one of my best friends, made it bearable, though. In 1995 she got me a job as a busgirl at Villa

Victoria. I needed money. Sometimes we'd sit around trying to think of ways to get money to buy booze.

One day at her house, I suggested donating blood. Jill said, "Let's just work." Our friend Carla's parents owned Villa Victoria.

Jill was a few grades under me, but she wasn't that far from my age. Jill was Slavic and tall. She had a nervous tic and was always shaking her leg, even when she was standing. She was thicker than the other girls and had a small space between her two front teeth. She had dark green eyes and full eyelashes. Her hair was blonde. Her skin was tan. Her eyebrows were dark brown. She was stunning and had no idea. She had a boyfriend who was in jail.

We rode around in her 1980 Jeep Cherokee, singing, "My baby just wrote me a letter," obviously referring to her incarcerated man. This same man would later beat up Jill and my (secret) girlfriend, Chloe, in the same night. When I tried to stop him, he threw me over his shoulder; I landed on my back, the wind completely knocked out of me. Sometimes my tailbone still hurts in that spot. But I loved Jill with all of my heart. For the time and the place where we grew up, she loved me back too. She never judged me for being gay. She supported everything I did. In a lot of ways, Jill protected me, even though she was usually the one who subjected us to danger.

Jill had sweet little dimples, and while she didn't know how stunning she was, she definitely knew how cool she was. She always wore long flowy skirts and tie-dyes. She wore lots of rings, bracelets, and jingly things so when she was bouncing her leg, she was always making some sort of music. She

loved the blues and the Grateful Dead. She laughed loud and wasn't afraid to be herself. I thought she was wild and free. She had opinions of her own and would argue for what she thought was right. And she was mostly right because she was good, all the way through.

Jill died in 2007. She died on the day of Chicago's stupid fucking South Side Irish Parade. She went to it with some friends, and after she got back to Indiana that night, the South Shore Line train rounded a corner and ran into her truck. Her friend Julie was in the passenger seat. I still can't listen to the Box Tops.

Little did I know when Jill walked me into Villa Victoria for a job, CCR playing from the bar and Frank Sinatra in the dining room, that I'd never leave this industry again. The place had green pleather booths, lots of thick dark wood beams, and mirrors. My mom took me there when we first moved to that dump of a neighborhood, full of upper-middle-class racist hillbilly assholes. I liked the restaurant, though. It's where I ate gnocchi for the first time.

I liked my dinner dates with my mom. She knew I loved food like she did. Every time she found something interesting or new in our tiny little town or the ones surrounding it, she took me there. My mom taught me things, like the time she tipped a waitress twenty dollars on a bill of fifty dollars. She said, "When service is good, you tip good. They will remember you forever and treat you like royalty the next time."

On my first day at work, I wore a crisp white button-up shirt, black slacks with pleats in the front, and shiny black wing tips. I looked nice, but everything was oversized. I

suppose I had never really learned how to dress. My mom dropped me off. I walked in the front door. I smelled garlic, stale booze, and smoke from the bar. No one told me how I should work or what I should do, but I did whatever they asked.

At work, I wanted to be the best. Basically, I taught myself work ethic; the desire to excel was built in. When it was busy, I hustled. When there was nothing to do, I cleaned. I hadn't often been the praised student in school. At this job, though, when I cleaned the dishes faster than anyone else, when I wrapped the shelves in new foil, everyone told me how hard of a worker I was and what a good job I was doing, and that made me feel really good.

The waitresses were nice. Dani, who was in her early twenties, drove a black T-top Camaro. She lived in a junky part of Hobart with her boyfriend. She liked to gossip. It was Dani who told me that Richard, the chef, was gay. Otherwise—even with his "gay" way of speaking—I wouldn't have known. But Dani was cool. Sometimes after work I'd have about ten dollars in tip money from the waitresses. Dani often drove me home, and we'd stop at the liquor store, where she'd buy me a cheap case of beer and a pack of Camels with my tips. Sometimes I didn't even let Dani tip me out just 'cause I knew we'd be going to the store afterward.

When it was slow, Richard would let me cook things on the line. Richard was only a little taller than me. At that time, I was already five-seven and lanky as hell. Richard would have been considered stocky. He had a beer belly and thick muscular arms. He was the first out gay person I ever met. He lived in Hebron, Indiana, a place that makes no sense

for a gay person to live in even today, let alone then. To top it off, he drove a red Ford Ranger, single cab, with a rainbow flag on the front. Most people who saw it around Hebron probably thought it meant Richard was happy or, more literally, liked rainbows. Being gay was still a little like being in a secret club that only those who knew really *knew*.

I didn't have any sort of gaydar back then. I was even a little homophobic but only because I was afraid of my own feelings.

I was curious about everything in the kitchen and asked lots of questions, and Richard showed me how it was done. Richard did the sort of cooking one did at a fancy restaurant in a small town. Rather than make a complex sauce out of deeply roasted bones, with lots of straining and reducing, he used tricks that chefs learned at the time. He mixed up cornstarch with a little water in his hand, rolled it into a ball, then tossed it into a broth of cheap Madeira cooking wine, chicken bouillon, water, and mushrooms. He added black pepper and lemon juice. Once the sauce was thick, he added in a few knobs of cold butter and swirled the pan efficiently over the burners. This sauce was then poured over roasted chicken and served with a side of spaghetti or gnocchi with your choice of marinara, Bolognese, or Alfredo. Yup, Alfredo, when that was still considered to be a part of Italian cuisine.

After work, I'd show Chloe these things in my kitchen, cooking my own versions of chicken Madeira, practicing the things I was learning. Other nights, though, I would have fun with Jill and Carla. Sometimes we'd steal a bottle of liquor from the banquet room and go to Carla's house since

her parents would still be closing down the bar. Carla's mom was usually drunk by the time she got home, so she didn't notice that we were drunk too, or she didn't care. In Carla's room, we danced to "Shakedown Street" and drank whatever we stole. We had officially started our restaurant careers.

Bon Femme Café, summer 1998. The tablecloths were faded and mismatched. Some were from old curtains or looked stolen, just unraveled from the fabric store, others were plastic. The lighting was dim and Merle Haggard was on the record player. A blue layer of cigarette smoke hung gently under the ceiling. Spider plants crawled up the front windows, letting in faint bits of light cut into webbed patterns against the carpeted floor. It was everything you want a country-style French café to be.

I was on my second bowl of French onion soup, which Bunny had taught me was the best, along with some specials of the day: raw oysters and bubbling buttered escargots served from special plates with little bowls. Bunny also had taught me to pile escargots high on thin slices of baguette.

Bunny had expensive taste, and when I visited her in Georgia, she introduced me to French food. She also introduced me to BBQ as it should be—prepared in a shack, the cooks sweating over pits outside, the fresh oysters popped with a screwdriver. Bunny always told me stories about the places we went, like how Allen's, which was supposed to have the best burger in Athens, was the first place the B-52s ever performed. I didn't like burgers back then, but I liked Allen's because it was special. I liked the BBQ because Bunny told

me BBQ was a family business; each generation had been making BBQ as soon as they got out of diapers. I fell in love with French onion soup at Bon Femme because she loved their bread and butter and scratchy record player. Bunny told me it was the best French onion soup in town.

When I finished my bowl of soup, I paid my check and left. That day I was eating alone, on my way home from Indiana University Northwest, where I was taking classes. That evening my sister Nina, who went to Bon Femme on her lunch breaks from the EMT house, said she had been there recently, too, and had asked them if they were hiring. She thought I'd fit in.

I had just quit the Chinese restaurant where I had been a delivery driver. I had learned to make crab Rangoon, chop suey, and lo mein noodles when we were slow.

That evening I drove back to Bon Femme. I parked in the back, where I always saw employees standing outside. I knocked on the door and poked my head in. Bubs had his hands in a large glob of dough. He had wiry hair, glasses, and a thin body with a firm, round belly. They called him Bubs 'cause of a habit he had—drinking Korbel Brut from a small Perrier bottle all day. His skin was olive, and he had on dark tortoiseshell frames around thick lenses that rested at the tip of his nose. He pushed them up with his forearm and asked, "What can I do to ya?" Right away: inappropriate but funny, and almost innocent.

Bubs was a father to a couple girls and a couple boys, and they all got good educations from Andrean High School, the same good Catholic high school I'd been sent to, and it wasn't cheap. Not that being a father makes you a good guy,

but he was a good guy and a good father, and it was easy to see that right away. When he released his hands from the dough, he held them over the garbage, dusted more flour on them, and then rubbed until the dough crumbled to little pieces and fell off. The few people who were working that night looked like hippies. They had a scent like Bunny when she came home after being gone a couple days following the Dead, or whatever she and Tom did.

I laughed. I was uncomfortable but also felt a little like I was home. It was warm and I could smell the caramelized onions and cheese as a burly hippie-looking dude with fiery red hair pulled a bowl of French onion soup from the toaster oven.

"You look hungry," Bubs said, maybe 'cause I was staring at the soup like a long-lost friend or maybe because at that time, I was one hundred pounds soaking wet. From the cocaine.

I had gotten a little on the heavier side by the end of high school from all the drinking. By then, I had also developed a darn good ability to cook for myself, just about anything I wanted. I was able to whip up more than a few Italian dishes. I could make fresh pasta. Chinese. I understood the beauty of MSG, something that was starting to become generally disliked, and I knew how to fill crab Rangoon to almost bursting. Cooking was becoming something I could do pretty well, and I was proud when I made things that others liked. I also felt proud when others said cooking was something they couldn't do. My sister Kelley, on several occasions, had told me I should go to cooking school instead of regular college.

Anyway, all of this led to a lot of eating. Then, because I

had gotten bigger, I got shamed. Not by my mother, who's had eating issues her whole life, but by Chloe, who told me her mom said I looked fat. The truth is, I wasn't—that's the real shame. However, I was bigger than I had ever been, 150 pounds, due to excessive drinking and eating.

The last time I remember eating something to comfort myself was when I stole a check from my mom's drawer and used it to buy Singapore rice noodles from the same Chinese restaurant where I one day worked. They noticed it was my handwriting on the check because they knew my mom, and later that evening, they called her. She was mad at me for stealing her money, even though it was for food. That night, I made a pledge to myself that I would get skinnier.

The next day, I started eating grapefruit for breakfast, a Lean Cuisine for lunch, and a piece of chicken breast or a small sandwich for dinner. If I drank, I did coke too, which prevented me from bingeing on food. I won't say it ever got bad enough, my monitoring my eating and bingeing, to develop an eating disorder, but I can see how one might get there, as was the case for many of my friends.

So one hundred pounds, apron wrapped around me twice, Bubs gave me a job as a line cook. It didn't take long for me to put on twenty pounds and get back to where I needed to be in terms of my natural weight.

The next morning, I started at ten. I was given a tour by Chili, the hippie guy with fiery red hair. He had a scruffy beard, as one does if you're a hippie. Chili would have been extremely handsome if not for his yellow and black teeth. He was tall, lean, and had very green eyes and all of that full, coarse red hair. He had a monstrous laugh and would tilt his

head back, almost as if in ecstasy, when laughing at anything Bubs said. Bubs was funny. They were characters.

At the cash register, Bubs funneled Korbel Brut into that small Perrier bottle that I learned was like an extension of his right hand, like the hook of Captain Hook. Chili showed me the chalkboard and told me what to write on it. He said that since I was a girl, by default I'd have better handwriting than him. Under *quiche*, he told me to write *Lorraine, broccoli and cheddar, spinach,* and *mushroom and Gruyère*. Under *salads,* he said, *asparagus with poppy seeds,* and *garden*. Under *crepes,* he said, *beef Bourguignon, chicken divan, bacon and onion*. Under *soups* were *French onion, potato and leek, black-eyed pea and ham, chicken,* and *pâte à choux dumpling,* which he told me was a French gnocchi. Under *pies* were *chocolate ganache, pecan,* and *tart cherry*. I didn't know how to spell some of these things, and Chili struggled with the spellings as well. He stated them out loud like a spelling bee, "Bourguignon, B-O-U-R-G" . . . thinking . . . "O-G-N-E."

The kitchen was tiny and dirty. Not in a filthy, rat-infested sort of way but just worn down, worked in, greased up. There was a stickiness to most of the counters that was either from sugar or dried-up oil and dust, maybe perhaps a little of both. By then I had learned to clean when I didn't know what else to do in a kitchen. But here there seemed no good place to start. I tried, though, and they said, "Luna, calm down. Lay off the coke." They teased me a lot, my being the youngest. They called me Luna—short for lunatic.

I was shoveled into the salad and dessert station. At eleven the doors opened for lunch. There I was in that nook, a thin white apron tied around my waist. A small shelf of

cookbooks sat above my station. There was a refrigerator with the salad mise en place and pies. Once orders came in, they showed me how to make everything one time, and after that I was on my own. It wasn't a sink-or-swim sort of place, but you had to catch on quick if you liked a station 'cause if you didn't, they'd just put you on dishwashing or waiting tables. It wasn't long before I was on both of those. But I took pride in my ability to wash dishes and even more pride in my ability to make guests happy. Back then it wasn't weird to smoke while waiting on tables. By noon there was usually a layer of blue smoke hovering near the ceiling, mostly from cigarettes. Whenever you pushed through the kitchen doors, whoever was on the hot line likely had spliffs hanging from their lips.

For the first few days, I stuck to myself, trying to not let anyone get to know me. I was uncomfortable. Also, by now I knew I was a handful. A lot of my friends had already warned me that if I kept up like I was, they were going to stop talking to me. I had barely enough energy to keep it together when I drank, but I did my best. Here, drinking seemed partly like a necessity, not a luxury. Both line cooks, including Bubs, were complete toast by the end of the day. Later, when I was coming in earlier to get my station set up exactly how I wanted it, and to clean a little, I realized that they often slept there.

Most days Chloe would show up toward the end of my shift. The line cooks liked Chloe. They liked to flirt with her. And she liked the attention. Chloe was wired to seek attention from men—and from women, like me. I don't know if it was something she was born with, some sort of natural talent,

or something else. But the truth is that it made my face turn red with anger that I tried desperately to hide. I hated every minute of it. I didn't know whether to compete with her or compete with the men. It made me hate her as much as I thought I loved her. I packed up my hate for them and her and put it in a little dark place in my heart.

We began to sleep there too. By this time, Chloe's mom had started thinking we didn't need to be sleeping over at each other's houses every night. Sometimes I'd sneak out of my house and run to hers. In the pitch dark, I'd enter her house through the basement, go up to the first floor, stalking in the dark. Then I crawled up the stairs to the second floor, minding every movement so as to not make anything creak, before I climbed into her bed. Most nights she was dead asleep. I lay there, blinking at the ceiling for a while, and then snuck back home. I don't know what I wanted because when we had sex, it was just me pleasuring her in some sort of way 'cause I didn't really know how sex worked yet. Chloe was never gay. Even though I wanted to believe differently, sometimes you just know these things.

Occasionally when we slept in the restaurant, we would make out as quietly as possible. If I woke up in the middle of the night, on the cold floor, I wouldn't find her next to me. After I adjusted my eyes to the dark, looking through the maze of table legs, I'd see her on the other side of the room, rocking back and forth over one of the guys. I wasn't allowed to say anything, nor was I able to stop it. We were still a secret. She told me she wasn't gay but that she liked me. I told her I wasn't gay but maybe I was bisexual, and she said, "No shit."

Chloe wasn't awful, even though this was agonizing. She was just a young girl with issues, something I'd chase for the rest of my life.

Bon Femme paid me twenty-five dollars a day. Chloe and I drank Captain Morgan. A half gallon was a little under twenty bucks. I worked, mainly, to buy us rum. Add a little for a little gas, then cigarettes, and that was really it. I was still at home so I didn't pay rent. I paid for a portion of my car payment. I was finally allowed to drive again since I was going to college. I abused that privilege every single day; I was nearly always a little tipsy when I was behind the wheel.

By then I had already had two drunk-driving accidents. One landed me in jail after I turned in front of an oncoming car. After the other, we went to the hospital before the police came and then home before they could catch up to us. My boyfriend at the time, Ben, was driving. Chloe and I had drunk a bunch of Jack Daniel's. Tom Petty was on the radio. "You're so bad," we were singing along when *smash*, the tires got stuck in a rut on the soft shoulder of the road and we slammed into that light post. I had a 1984 Crown Victoria; heavy and long, the size of it is probably what saved our lives. The front of the car was like an accordion, the dashboard nearly touching our chests. We could all sit in the front because it had bench seating. We slid out, one by one, into the ditch. The ambulances came and swooped us away.

I don't remember what day it was when I met Sarah. I know a couple days before I met her, I waited on her. She had come in to eat and sat at a small table with a woman who even I

at the time thought looked very much like a lesbian—pretty but with short hair, like a crew cut, and she was not wearing a lot of makeup. I felt them looking at me, a lot, even when my back was turned. I knew I was being checked out. For the first time, I experienced women openly, unabashedly flirting with me. I was sort of shocked and also curious. It felt nice.

I'd had encounters, flirting with women. That's what had led to the relationship Chloe and I were in. This was way different, though.

When I came to the table, Sarah rested her chin in her hand. She looked like Scarlett Johansson. Her cheekbones were high and round, her lips full and pink, and her eyes were like big turquoise balls under slightly arched brows. Sarah was blonde but not like how people stereotype blondes. She looked sweet, like a girl next door, and also intelligent.

The next day I came in, hung over as usual, and set up the dining room. I lit the candles on the tables, hit the power button on the coffee maker, and finished drawing little flowers in chalk on the board. The bells on the front door chimed and Merle Haggard's janky guitar started from the record player. It was Sarah. She looked nervous. She asked if we were hiring.

"Hold on," I said, and I went to the back.

I had butterflies in my stomach. If I had kept a diary back then, I might have written how "Sarah makes me all fluttery. It's strange that I feel this way when I think I'm in love with Chloe. But Chloe is such a *jerk* to me! And we have to pretend we are not together. Sarah goes out to dinner with lesbians, so I'm sure she's just fine being out of the closet, if that's what she is. I think Sarah is coming to the restaurant for me." I'd write about how pretty she was and how "I didn't notice it at first.

It took everyone else to fawn over her to realize that this girl who was so pretty actually likes me."

I was an idiot, and I said stupid things, and every day I told myself to have a better filter, but it just didn't work, not with a pint of rum in me anyway. Most of the time, I thought everyone was as drunk as I was, but they weren't.

I asked Bubs if we were hiring. I told him he should see Sarah first before he said we weren't. Once he saw her, he asked if she could start tomorrow. So that was it. Sarah was going to work with us, and I was going to understand more about what it meant to actually be gay.

August 1998. 9 p.m. I sat naked on Chloe's cold basement floor. It was dark but for three candles in front of me. Chloe was to my right, and Sarah was in front of me, the jam box was to my left. It was Sarah's idea to get naked. Candles, the screen door to outside open, a steady breeze coming through. Chloe's parents gone. Velvet Underground sang "Sweet Jane" softly through the speakers of the tape player. I was eighteen that day. I didn't feel different. Actually, I was scared.

The femme fatale could have been any one of us, but I was least likely to know that about myself.

Sarah was very confident. Sarah knew how attractive she was, and she didn't care. Chloe knew she was attractive and did care. The attention she got from men was something she needed.

I didn't want to get naked, but they had encouraged me, and it might have been more awkward had I sat there with my

clothes on. They told me I had a nice body, but I wasn't sure. I had an idea of what that was supposed to look like, based on images of women's bodies in magazines, and I knew I wasn't that. I didn't really care though—at least, not too much.

They finished a joint, and we were a third of the way through a half gallon of spiced rum.

"We should get some coke," I said.

Sarah rolled her eyes. She didn't like coke. But Chloe was into it.

"We don't have money for that," Chloe said. "If my dad was here, I'm sure we could steal enough cash." Chloe took money from her dad's wallet all the time. Sometimes she'd swipe a hundred and we'd go to Miller Beach and have a nice dinner: bread with butter and roasted garlic, escargots, oysters on the half shell, Nicoise salad, roasted duck, and berries with vanilla cream.

"You guys need some feminism in your music life," Sarah said and slipped an Ani DiFranco tape into the jam box. Ani played a rough rhythm on the guitar strings, and her voice was like a rapture, lesbian fire and brimstone. We listened for a while and talked more.

One of the candles burnt out. We were all very drunk. At least I was. Sarah put her hand on my leg, and Chloe touched my boob while kissing my neck. I felt weird. I thought I loved Chloe. And I was definitely intrigued by Sarah. But if I were to have either one of them, it would have been separately. Not like this. I sobered for a second, jumped up, and grabbed my jeans from the old sofa where we usually sat to play Contra in front of the television. I pulled them on hurriedly, off-balance, didn't even zip them before I grabbed

my shirt and walked out the back. I lit a cigarette and walked around the side of the house.

The grass outside was already wet with dew. My bare feet sank. Chloe's dad had been traveling a lot, and her brother was lazy and didn't keep the yard up, even though he was supposed to. Sometimes we partied with him and his girl-friend. His girlfriend was warm and loving and squishy. She had the most beautiful face and emerald-green eyes and long black hair; we could never figure out why she liked him, other than he had the boyish good looks of the Beatles. But imagine Paul McCartney without him being a Beatle—*just* cute, sorta. Anyway, I thought about this as I walked to the front stoop of the house and sat down. I thought about going home, but I didn't want to leave. I didn't want to leave Chloe alone with Sarah. I didn't trust either of them together. Probably right at that moment, Chloe was try-ing something with her or the other way around. It wasn't worth going back in and finding out.

But I also didn't want to leave Sarah. I was interested in her. At work one evening as we sat in booth one, the em-ployee booth, which was covered in ashtrays and beer bottles, she told me that in Bloomington, where she went to college, it was normal for people to be out and gay. There were even gay and lesbian bars. Sarah made me feel sort of normal.

The sun had just set, and we walked from the dunes, flash-light guiding us, single file: Chili, Chloe, Sarah, then me. We walked to our campsite, set up the tent, and built a bon-fire. By that light we listened to music powered by battery,

roasted s'mores, and drank whiskey. Chloe and Chili were uncomfortably close, and I couldn't do anything about it. I couldn't out us. He knew her brother, and her brother would for sure tell her parents. Sarah and I seemed to care the most, as we watched him nuzzle his wiry beard and mouth against her neck. She sat between his legs, his arms around her, and leaned into him. His raucous laugh echoed through the trees.

When they went into the tent, Sarah and I sat silent for a little bit. As we heard things inside the tent begin to rustle, Sarah tapped my arm and said, "Let's get out of here." I had driven everyone and at that exact minute did not give a fuck that I was stranding Chili and Chloe there.

Sarah said we should drive to Chicago, so we did. I had about ten bucks in my pocket. Sarah paid for gas and tolls. At about ten, we pulled up at 2625 Halsted Street. There was a three-story home, or what looked like a home, painted dark. A small neon sign in the bay window along the first floor read, "Girl Bar." My first *real* lesbian bar. My first *real* time being around other women like me.

I felt my shoulders curl as I entered using Sarah's state ID while she used her driver's license. I waited to go in until after several girls had gone between us, hanging out a few doors down, smoking a cigarette in a gangway, peeking around the corner like some sort of private investigator.

I didn't drink as much as I would have in order to feel comfortable or to talk to anyone, while Sarah pointed out girls she thought were cute. I responded with, "She seems a little goth," or "She seems a little edgy." There was a quiet girl who sat alone wearing black leather pants and shirt, glasses, and very red lipstick. She had spiked hair. Sarah talked to her

for a while as I watched women play pool, better than most men I had seen, and pretended to be interested.

That night we drove back to Sarah's aunt's house, where she was staying for the summer. She told me I could stay over, but I refused. I waited for her to get in the house, then sat for a minute, beating myself up. I killed the ignition, then lightly knocked, as it was already three in the morning and I didn't want to wake the rest of the family.

Sarah opened the door and laughed at me. "So *now* you want to stay over?"

"Yeah," I said sheepishly.

Alas, nothing happened that night. Instead she broke the news that she was going back to Bloomington, and soon. But she said that I should come with her. I could share her room until I eventually got my own place, and she'd get me a job at the pizza place where she worked.

Back home, my mom and dad had already been split up for a year, for the last time. My mom was moving to Chicago to work at Bloomingdale's; she had found a one-bedroom apartment. We were in our kitchen when she casually said she was going, with or without me, while she cracked open a can of beer. Within a couple weeks, I was going to be homeless.

I told Sarah yes.

It's funny how you'll remember people for the rest of your life because, in some way, they saved you, even though you didn't know it at the time. It was my love of that French onion soup that took me to Bon Femme, my *lesbian essence* that intrigued Sarah, and Sarah's empathy that got me the fuck out of all of it. One more step further away from being the transgender, big rig–driving carny I was born to be.

—

Mother Bear's Pizza. Bloomington, Indiana. Fall 1998. First semester.

"I have herpes," Jason said. Jason had a scrawny ponytail and freckles. His teeth were crooked but he wasn't terrible-looking, just not what you would call cute. Or any other synonym like that. We sat in the dark on the back steps of Mother Bear's while the delivery drivers whizzed past us, feeding hungry college students. We drank beer out of waxed paper cups that read "Pepsi" on the side. We used lids and straws, trying to disguise it, and even put ice in the cups so it sounded like soda. "My girlfriend knows. We use protection, but it makes it complicated for children. You know?"

"No," I said, not really knowing what herpes was.

"Well, if you have sex with herpes unprotected, you can give it to your girlfriend."

"What is it?"

"It's a sore that comes on every once in a while."

"Well, I'm sure if she loves you, then you'll figure it out."

Sarah walked out and lit a cigarette. She waited tables wearing a jean skirt with an apron that made her look like she wasn't wearing a skirt at all. She had on old Nikes and a flannel. A bandana held her hair back and was tied in a knot at the top of her head. She didn't like Jason. Jason was a townie, meaning he didn't go to school but had grown up in Bloomington. I didn't mind him. He got us beer, and he showed me how to bloom yeast and make hundreds of pizza crusts in a single batch. That was our job. We made pizzas for all the dorms. Each day we'd make hundreds

of pizzas, and they'd be picked up the next morning and shipped out.

Another guy, Chris, worked in the back with us. He was in charge. Chris was a tall, skinny Chinese guy with acne. It didn't matter what Jason or I ever wanted to listen to; when Chris came in, he put in a Sublime tape, the same one, and that was what we listened to. He repeated facts about the lead singer's death from heroin. Every day. I guess it was a pretty good band. I grew to like them after I knew every single lyric.

Sarah stood there and smoked. Jason didn't really talk to her because he knew he couldn't talk to girls like her. But I wasn't one of those girls, and if I was, I didn't know it. So I told him about Chloe and explained what happened.

"Chloe and I are still *together*," I said making air quotes. "We fought that day at the dunes. When I got home from Sarah's the next day, she was waiting in my driveway. I laughed uncomfortably when I saw her standing there. This is a behavior I learned from my dad. You know how it is when you do something, and you know exactly where it came from? I think my dad did the same thing when my mom found out he was cheating on her. The whole way home, I had been flying down the country roads blasting Diana Ross on repeat."

"Yeah, I love Diana Ross," Jason said.

I looked at Sarah, like, *That's endearing*. But she rolled her eyes and looked away. "She was laughing back at me, though I realized it was fake when she reached into the car and grabbed me by the neck. This wasn't a great day, as I had stranded her at the beach. But I had learned a new boundary called taking care of myself, and I was jumping at the

opportunity to move to Bloomington. As messy as it all was, I was still doing something better than staying there."

"Fuck yeah," Jason said, "Bloomington is the best city in Indiana."

"It's hardly a city," Sarah interjected, and threw her cigarette butt in the gravel. She walked in and I squished it with my sneaker.

I continued, "At the end of the night, we had decided this was the best thing for us, for both of us really. Maybe we were hoping the time apart would allow us to be the people we really were."

"Are you a different person? Or a better person? Now?" he asked.

"I don't know. She's coming to visit this weekend," I said, "so I guess not."

Chris came out back. "Break's up," he said. He bummed a cigarette from Jason and we went in. I asked Chris if I could sauce the pizzas or add the toppings, which was usually his job, or Jason's job if he wasn't there.

"Nope," he said, with all the weighty pride of a *Legend of Zelda* champion. "You're not there yet."

Chapter 9
Tequila

TEQUILA MAKES ME GO TO JAIL. I TELL PEOPLE THIS and they laugh. But it's true.

January 21, 2001. I woke up in the tank. The lights were a low-wattage fluorescent, a bunch of bugs dead on them. The stench was like sour gym socks and a thirteen-year-old boy's bedroom, although no boys were present. My face hurt. My nose cracked as I wiped it with the back of my hand; dried cocaine from the morning before flaked off. I felt miserable. Bones hurt, skin hurt, brain hurt. Serotonin long gone. At first, I hadn't the vaguest recollection of where I was, and I hoped for a second it was all some twisted nightmare. Could I just be in my bed? I squinted my dry eyes. Everything was gray.

I rolled onto my back and it felt like a million nails rather than the buttons of my spine. I dared look down the length of my body. Some of the stench was coming from a

bit of dried puke on my new sweater. My pants were torn at the knees with road rash on them. My shoes and socks were off. I wondered if I had killed someone.

I searched my memory, using it like a file cabinet, pulling the drawers out, manila folders flying everywhere. There was the coke; the guy with the red hair I called Ginger; Tammy, my best friend, begging me to leave with her; my refusal. Then the guy's apartment and him showing me pictures of his trip to Africa. He looked like Sean Penn. His other friend was with him. I thought they might hurt me, but they didn't. Did I hurt them? The smell of the metal key. Snorting coke. The bar that opened at 8 a.m. The Mexican restaurant, tequila, then complete blackness. I touched my leg and then my wrists.

The police had pulled up outside the restaurant, lights flashing. I had an ache in my wristbones from the tight handcuffs. I had tried to run. As it was late morning by then, it had gotten bright and sunny. This was in Lincoln Park, on Lincoln Avenue just north of DePaul University. Running.

I ran down the yellow line splitting the road. Officially a crazy lady running in handcuffs. It was the first day in weeks that we'd hit a high of forty degrees. Patches of ice were melting, and I fell, facedown, and skidded down the street, my body along the yellow line splitting the road. My hands were behind my back, the flesh over my cheekbone scraped away.

The police car ride, unpleasant. I kicked the seats, shouting names at the officers: "Lesbian cop. Dick-sucking whore. Big fat motherfucking child molester. Doughnut-eating piece of shit. Sticking long johns in your asshole. Killer!"

At the station, I folded forward in a chair across from an officer, my pants undone, humiliated after mug shots and a body check. I guess I was offered a phone call and I declined.

Back in the cell block, I yelled for help. "Can't I get a call?" I screamed. I thought I'd call Tammy or my mom. A few cells down, a lady told me to shut up.

"They ain't going to help you," a raspy voice said from a dark corner of the cell. Terri was her name. She loomed, shadowy, above the toilet. She farted.

I quickly turned away and called for help again. It was dark already and must have been well into the evening, whether the same day or the next, I had no idea. Finally a guard came down.

"What?" she said.

"Do I get a phone call?"

"Nope."

I wondered if I had made one. "Did I make one?"

"Paper here says you refused."

All I could think about at the moment was calling my mom, going to her apartment, getting cleaned up, and starting my life over. A promise I'd made to myself before when I'd been behind bars and then broken again within hours of freedom. Even if it came with disappointment, I just wanted my mom so I could feel safer. I'd sit on her couch with her, and we'd watch *Law & Order*. She loved that show.

"How can I leave?"

"When your prints are cleared."

"How long does that take?"

"Anywhere from one to twenty-four hours. They get sent downtown, and we need to make sure we don't have to keep you for anything else."

"I haven't done anything else," I said, not even knowing what I had done in the first place.

The guard disappeared and Terri, in the corner, tried to talk to me again, but I just took a roll of toilet paper from the shelf, wrapped what I could around my feet, then put the rest under my head as a pillow. I silently cried as I worried about what in the hell I had done to get there. Why was I so determined to escape from the police? Why had I done this again?

Terri talked and talked about herself. I tried to drown her out, but it was actually better just to listen. I thought about how in ten years, I could be her: with a few kids whose whereabouts I wouldn't know. I'd live in a tent under Lawrence and Lake Shore Drive.

I had been held like this once before, over a holiday when I had crashed my mom's car—for the second time. I knew what I had done that time. I was sixteen. One snowy November day on a dark country road, I turned to go over a tiny bridge. Another car was headed toward us as I crossed lanes. I thought it was far enough away. I thought I could make it.

The impact was strong. Airbags and white dust exploded. Rick, who I loved to listen to Beastie Boys with—yeah, well, he ran. Chloe was hit the hardest and got a scrape on her arm, but we were OK. The cops came, and that was it. My mom's car was totaled. They took Chloe home. I was taken to juvenile detention.

I remember the long letter I wrote my parents the next night. I was in an observation cell for the accident and was so upset with myself they thought I was suicidal. I was sobbing

loud and uncontrollably, and a kid on the other side of the wall kept saying I'd be all right and not to worry. I was crying so much. His consolation was not consoling. I didn't feel better. Once I realized crying wasn't going to do anything but make me feel worse, I asked him questions. Like why was he there? Had he been there before? What was his name?

This kid, Jimmy, was only twelve and had anger issues. The more he talked, the worse I felt for him, as opposed to myself. I had been a negligent brat and asshole, while he truly had problems—no parents around, a grandma who was sort of mean to him, a sister in a foster home.

In my letter, I promised my parents and myself that I'd never drink again. Now here I was, six years later, drinking myself into cocaine, handcuffs, and another jail cell.

After what seemed like several more hours but could have been minutes, the guard called to me, "Regan, get your boots. Let's go."

My boots were outside of the cell. They took me to a desk and gave back to me the things I'd had with me—keys, wallet. They had me sign a slip of paper that had a code signifying my offense, as well as a court date.

"Where am I?" I asked the woman at the desk. She made some kind of internal sigh or groan, then tilted her head, disgruntled, and said, "Belmont and Western."

I stepped out into the city darkness. Streetlights shone orange on the wet, cold pavement. Whatever warmth had been there that morning, or the morning before, was gone now. It was 10 p.m. I walked out to what appeared to be the busiest street, Western, and flagged a cab.

When I got to my apartment, I asked the driver to just

wait out front so that I could run up and get him a check. He was pissed at that and insisted on waiting in my vestibule. Now, there was no way I was going to let this guy walk in my building behind me. Had he had drugs with him the night before, though, without a doubt I would have invited him in; maybe I'd have even let him crash, offered him a beer, and shared my life story with him. I'm sure I reeked of jail and stale alcohol, and I had that large gash on my face. Now here I was, acting afraid of my cab driver. I promised I'd be right back down.

Once inside, I scrambled to find my checkbook. I wrote him a check that I knew would bounce. I knew it would take at least three days for the check to clear, so I wasn't really worried about it.

I was so happy I was home. I listened to my messages. One was from Tammy, wondering if I was OK. The other was from Ginger, checking in as well. I suppose that was nice. For a second, I thought about calling him to find out what had happened. Instead I called Tammy and left a message: "Hey, I'm OK. Long story. I'll come see you tomorrow."

Tammy had set me up with a therapist whom she really trusted. She was a cool lady, it seemed. She's where Tammy learned, and then taught me, to ask, "What are you waiting for? Permission? You won't get it, so you just have to do it." I'd end up turning to that again and again. I guess if anyone helped shape me into who I am today, it was Tammy. When I was broke, she told me to find better jobs. When I was unhappy with school, she told me to change my major.

I met with the therapist, Alyssa, a couple of times in her basement. The first time, I felt uncomfortable talking about

my family and stuff because I really felt like nothing was wrong there. People who go to a therapist, I thought, were people with real trauma. I hadn't experienced that. Tammy had been through a life of abuse—a drunk mom, multiple stepfather fill-ins after her dad died. She'd dated guys who were mean, who tried to hit her for things like not opening the blinds in the morning. That wasn't part of my story. I mean, you understand, it wasn't perfect, and everyone in my family was a bit fucked up, but I hadn't endured abuse—at least not bad enough to cause me to be the asshole I sometimes was or to make the terrible decisions I so often made. I was scheduled to meet with Alyssa again in the morning. Perfect timing, since I had so royally fucked up.

After I listened to the messages, I went to the bathroom and turned on the shower. As the steam rose over the shower walls, I carefully pulled my jeans down over the bruises on my legs. My bones still hurt, and I had to slowly twist the sweater over my head. I added it to my pile of dry cleaning. In the mirror, I tended to the road rash on my face, first treating it with peroxide. White bubbles sizzled over the sore where it hadn't scabbed yet. I winced. Then I took a long hot shower and went to bed.

The next day, my body didn't feel any better. Aside from the bruises from the handcuffs, I had escaped this incident with the gash on my cheek as the only real visible story. I got dressed. In my kitchen, I heated up a pot of water and added a couple spoonfuls of powdered coffee. I put it in a thermos and left. It was cold again. I cursed myself for wasting the one nice sunny January day in a jail cell, sleeping off cocaine and tequila. I took the bus to Tammy's

house. I had the slip of paper from the jail crumpled in the pocket of my peacoat.

When I got there, she made me another cup of coffee. Tammy liked African coffee because of all the time she had spent there studying anthropology. Her long dreads were pulled up in a high bun at the top of her head. Her eyes were sympathetic as she set the mug of coffee in front of me. Then she sat at the kitchen table and laughed at me, loudly. Whatever. She sat across from me, and I slid the crumpled piece of paper across the table to her. There was a number there, and she said she'd call, pretending to be me. It was easier that way. Maybe if I had called on my own, the shame would have settled deeper, taught me a lesson.

"Hi, yes, I'll hold." She stuck her tongue out at me, then adjusted her septum ring. "Yes." She was very professional-sounding. "I was in jail last night, and I can't remember what happened or how I got there.

"Yes, there's a number, it's . . ." and she read the number. I wiggled, uncomfortable in my chair. "Thank you." She hung up the phone. I remember it was one with a rotary dial.

She looked at me. "Bad news. You are going to be going back to jail for a long, long time."

Panic set in. "What did I do?"

"Well . . ." she started, as my eyes filled with tears, then she busted out laughing. "Nothing! Just public intoxication. You'll go to this court date, and the person who called the cops on you probably won't even press charges. But *do not* miss this date." She threw the paper back at me.

"I won't." Though I couldn't *really* be sure.

We sat on her porch, which was just an enclosed staircase,

and we smoked a couple of cigarettes. She put on the CD of a singer who was auditioning to perform at a festival she was organizing for later that year, at the end of the summer. The music was twangy and the angelic voice and words were amazing, sad, soulful. This was Neko Case.

"What are you going to do today?"

"I've got to meet Alyssa."

"Good."

I liked to walk even though it was cold. There was something about the silence in the bitter cold, just the automobiles crunching over snow and ice. I set one foot in front of the other. I was just all sorts of fucked. I could sort of still hear Neko Case echoing in my head. Alyssa's house was in the next neighborhood. Wicker Park to Bucktown. I arrived about a half hour early. There was a restaurant across the street, so I stopped in and thought I'd have a snack. I had eight bucks left. They were just about to open. I sat at the bar.

I never made it back to Alyssa. I didn't go that day or any other day. There was a bartender there, a cute girl, and she kept talking to me, and I kept drinking 'cause she kept pouring. She said she lived in my neighborhood, so that night I rode the train home with her. We had to walk about a mile to get to the train, but she was a walker like me—we bundled up. I was already drunk again.

As we walked, I clumsily tried to kiss her or hold her hand. At this point, whatever she might have found attractive about me was gone. I slurred my words, stumbled, proudly relayed my jail story, like it was some badge of honor being a bad girl, spending the night locked up. Note: public intoxication does not make for a cute story later for why you landed

in jail. Maybe if it had been grand theft or running a chop shop, that would have been something.

Somehow, in my crossed double vision, I managed to see a sign outside of what looked like an abandoned building: "Liar's Club." How apropos. It was glowing.

"Hey," I stopped and leaned against the building. "This is where Ginger bartends. What is today?"

"Monday," she said. I grabbed her by the arm and dragged her inside. We took a seat at the bar.

I looked at the bartender; if it had been a lineup I would have had no idea who the guy was. But he noticed me. I was a baby-faced twenty-one-year-old with high cheekbones, angular eyebrows, and a shaved head.

"Oh my God. Never thought I'd see you again," he said sweetly, a bit of relief in his voice.

I was searching for guilt in his face—as if I was in a position to determine something like that—but his story was as follows: "You were drunk as shit. Couldn't even stand or see. You were starting to fall asleep at the table. You got up to go to the bathroom and when you came back, you started throwing food at us and yelling. They told us we had to leave. You kept demanding more shots of tequila. We took you outside and tried to get you into a cab, and you started fighting with us. When you started throwing punches, the cops showed up. Once you started running, we just got the fuck out of there."

He bought me and the girl each a beer, and when I ordered a shot, he looked at me and said, "You can't do shots, better go home instead." We finished our beers and left.

The train was full of normal people headed home, noses

in books, magazines, things like that. It was now about nine in the evening. The girl told me to keep my voice down. Supposedly she was a model when she wasn't tending bar. She was pretty, but I wasn't always the best judge of those things. All I could think about was not being alone. I felt afraid. I insisted on walking her home. I attempted a few more times to kiss her, thinking maybe I'd get company for the night. It wasn't about sex—that would have been terrible, drunk as I was. I just couldn't imagine what I'd do next. It was sort of about safety. Someone watching me. All my attempts at maintaining her company completely failed.

Luckily, her apartment wasn't that far from mine. I walked the rest of the way home and somehow managed not to stop at another bar to finish myself off. I made it home, and my roommate, Carl, was asleep on the futon. I hadn't seen him in days. I lay down on the floor next to the futon and passed out.

For the next couple days, I carried on as normally as I could. A phone call with Elizabeth ended up going out via carrier pigeon or something like that, and suddenly my whole family knew I'd been in jail again. But no one had much to say to me about it—there were some messages checking in, and my mom asking me if I'd like to have dinner. That was always her way to get to me, a nice meal. So I set something up with her. She wanted to take me to a restaurant owned by lesbians. I blushed. I went to my classes, and on the second day after I was back to life without bars, went to work.

I worked at what I thought was an upscale Vietnamese French restaurant, and I guess it was. Mimi's Viet Brasserie

was cute, and it was only about three blocks from my apartment. I still had a scrape across my upper right cheek like a football player's eye black, and I was smoking a cigarette as I reached the front door. Mimi had her arms folded across her chest and was watching out the window. The snow fell around her reflection in the glass. I threw my cigarette down.

Without looking at me as I walked in, Mimi said, "You smell."

I thought she meant the smoke, but she could have meant alcohol from the night I went to jail. It was still coming from my pores.

Mimi was mean. She was tall and stood even taller because of her Coach stilettoes. I felt small next to her. She was sort of like a Vietnamese Cruella de Vil. I didn't have dogs back then, but if she could have skinned my dogs for coats, she would have. She liked to entertain men at night—not like a hooker, I mean she just liked being with the boys. I'd have to stay late while they all sat at tables in the front half of the restaurant, near the bar. They played card games. Gambling with real money. The room thick with blue smoke. *Why the fuck did she shame me for smoking when the whole place was smoked out?*

I sat at the bar in between serving them. I read a book on bartending and studied the drinks. It was an old book with old-fashioned drinks. There were no new, fun drinks that people wanted, like apple martinis or things like that. I didn't know at the time how useful this would become, but I couldn't just sit there, and every time I brought homework like biochem or statistics to the restaurant, Mimi made me put my books away. So I just stopped bringing it altogether.

I had to work. At the time, I was studying chemical engineering and not doing too well, either. It was hard to make it to classes.

Most of the time, the Brasserie was slow. The only busy night I ever remember was one Valentine's Day. I served about fifteen bottles of Santa Margherita pinot grigio that night.

There was another woman who was also a server, Jackie. She was younger and shorter than Mimi and very pretty. She was nice to me. She asked me what had happened to my cheek, but I didn't tell her. She looked at me sympathetically and told me stories about her friends who were lesbians. But she called them "resbians," making air quotes with her long, painted nails every time she said it: "resbian." We both laughed.

Nam and Dam worked in the kitchen. They were two old Vietnamese grandmas, sisters, but they didn't look similar except for their height, hair color, and eyes. They were both nice but a little leery of me. *Nam* and *Dam* meant "five" and "eight." That was the only story Mimi ever told me, and I think it was to shame them rather than give me background.

As Nam and Dam began to trust me more, they began to teach me things. They taught me how to make Vietnamese spring rolls, how to cook Dungeness crab, and how to make their version of French onion soup. They showed me how to make pho broth and taught me the importance of the spices.

I learned how to communicate with these women through food because we couldn't say much of anything else. When Mimi wasn't there, I'd hoist myself up onto the prep table and they'd feed me whatever they were eating for lunch that day. They often came waddling down the street,

their eyes peering from under winter hats but above full brown grocery bags from Tai Nam, which was about four blocks down the road. Sometimes I stood outside to wait for them, exhaling smoke and cold breath, then helped them carry in the fresh fruits and vegetables of all shapes and colors. I once held dragon fruit with its fuchsia skin and little yellow hairs, like *what the?* Then they took it from me, cut it open, and fed me a slice. It was like inadvertently applying lip stain.

Later, Jackie teased me, "Ripstick resbian." And we fucking cracked up. It was a nice job when Mimi wasn't there.

Nam and Dam liked to watch me eat, and I think they were thrilled that this white girl liked all the spices they used in everything. When I started, the kitchen there was filthy. When there was time, I changed the foil they used to cover the bottom shelves of their prep tables, or I scrubbed the wall by the dish station. I cleaned the tracks of the sliding refrigerator doors. I guess it was both a blessing and curse that I saw these things needed to be cleaned when others did not even notice. This is something that has haunted me—and my employees—ever since. I've heard it said that's what Charlie Trotter was like, always asking for some of the strangest things to be cleaned, like light switches. I completely understand. I mean, my mom wouldn't let me wash my hands in the kitchen sink 'cause she didn't want water drops in it, you understand. It was just one of those things. Like ironing my socks.

I learned that working like this, cleaning or just helping with a little extra care and elbow grease, could take me a long way from the Italian restaurant of my teens. Maybe it

was because Dani, Richard, and Carla's parents praised me so much when I worked hard. But I also saw it got me things other than praise—in this case, it got Mimi off my back. She was always storming into the kitchen, eyes fierce and flickering back and forth, looking for a reason to yell at me. But if I was cleaning, she'd quickly turn and walk away.

I eventually quit the Brasserie one afternoon. It was slow, and I was scrubbing the bottom of an aluminum stockpot that was black from the stove. Mimi banged through the swinging doors so hard they rattled. She yelled in Vietnamese at Nam and Dam. I felt myself shrinking the way a turtle pulls its head into its shell. I ducked past her and through those doors. I grabbed my coat and book bag and walked out.

I had done this before, simply disappeared from a place without notice. What did it matter? As much as I knew I was good when I wanted to be, I also knew I was a cog in the machine. It wasn't a good thing. I didn't know how to communicate very well, but would it have even been worth it, sitting Mimi down and trying to tell her she hurt my feelings? She might have only laughed in my face, "Oh ho ho, I hurt your feelings! *What* feelings, you smelly girl?" So there.

Once more, I heard the rattle and bang of the kitchen doors. "Where are you going?" Mimi yelled.

I didn't answer her. I pulled my jacket collar up around my ears. I walked north up Clark Street to Simon's Tavern, where they knew me. They'd seen me in the corner passing out into my beer more than once. They never bothered me, and I always seemed to make it home safely. There was Schlitz for a dollar.

I had ten dollars in my pocket, a term paper due on the

Krebs cycle, and that big scratch on my face from my attempt at resisting arrest. I had quit my job, again, and I had nothing else lined up.

At least I knew how to make spring rolls, pho, Vietnamese French onion soup, and classic cocktails. I knew how Vietnamese men liked to drink Bia Ha Noi over ice—and someday I'd get to Hanoi myself, I knew.

Most importantly, though—I would drink tequila no more. And I actually did keep that promise.

Chapter 10
Trio

November 3, 2002. Nathan, Michael, and I smooshed ourselves inside the tiny, dirty bathroom. I sat on the toilet tank with my feet on the seat. Michael had the key to his Chevy Malibu in a little baggie of coke. He had one of those devil goatees and it looked stupid. Nathan leaned against the sink. He wasn't going to do any coke, but if I was alone with another guy, he wanted to make sure he was there. He didn't trust me. Rightly so. I didn't trust myself either. Chloe was at home sleeping. For some reason, though, that didn't matter to him; he didn't care about me being with Chloe. He only cared when I was around other guys (somehow, I really understand this). Honestly, Chloe sleeping at home didn't really matter to me either. Not that I wanted or loved Nathan, by any means. I thought I loved Chloe. I figured sometimes fucking around with Nathan meant nothing. Most of the time I felt unwanted anyway,

so I liked the attention. It was usually Chloe who fucked every guy in sight, behind my back or in front of me. What was the difference if I cheated on her now?

"This place is sort of disgusting," I said.

Michael put the key up to my nostril. I pushed my knuckle against the other side of my nose and inhaled as hard as I could.

In proper dad fashion, Nathan said, "She doesn't like coke; she just likes the smell of it." He laughed, trying to be sarcastic but also mean at the same time. He didn't like when I did coke. It was a thing by then, even though I didn't want it to be a thing. I had escaped it once before when I moved to Bloomington, but now here it was again, like an old teddy bear I thought I got rid of but then found again, and all the nostalgia came back. Coke was my teddy.

"What do you care?" I asked.

"I have all the cares," he replied in his standard puppy dog fashion, turning on me the largest brown eyes I had ever seen. He was tall and thin with high cheekbones and olive skin. He was really pretty for a boy. I liked Nathan a lot but not enough to be in any kind of relationship. Every time I slept with a guy I felt violated, even if it was sweet and gentle. I can't explain it, but maybe I don't need to.

Anyway, coke was better than sex, as far as I was concerned. Like drinking, I would get turned on just thinking about it. As wound up as it made me, it also relaxed me—as if every part of me that usually wanted to crawl out of my skin had instead snuggled into bed and turned out the light. No bogeymen, no monsters, no nightmares—just sweet comfort, myself inside myself exactly as I am. Sweet, sweet coke.

Three loud thumps sounded against the door above the music and buzzing in our brains. Michael and I were perfectly jacked up, like we were transforming from a couple of Clark Kents to Supermen, right there. Nathan gulped down a full beer and tossed it near the trash can.

We squeezed back out into the party, and the guy with the fist mumbled, "Queers."

"Nathan and Michael are not queers!" I yelled. They were cute, young, and clean-cut for the most part. Me, my head was still shaved and, well, I'd heard this before.

We settled against a wall and proceeded to eat our lower jaws while jabbering about everything culinary we could think of. We were inspired by our boss, a young chef named Grant Achatz. We worked at what we thought—what we knew—was one of the best restaurants in the United States, a small place in Evanston, just north of Chicago, called Trio.

Two nights before, I had been on the phone with Elizabeth. I sat on the kitchen floor with my back against the wall. I had just left work. I wore a pair of pin-striped slacks with a creased front that I had purchased for my interview at Trio. I lit a cigarette. I told her about one of the dishes, a Bloody Mary on a plate. She couldn't believe it. "Yeah, so it's this tomato that they confit."

"What's confit?"

"Well, typically, that's something cooked in its own fat until it's tender and falls from the bone." I took a drag from my cigarette, feeling smart. "In this case, they cook the tomato in olive oil very gently, until it's very soft but still intact."

"Uh-huh," she said, listening with intent.

"Then there's a celery granita, which is like a shaved ice.

There's cubes of Worcestershire gel, and black pepper, and red wine vinaigrette, and then we spray vodka on it."

"How do you do that?" she asked. "It's incredible," she said before I could finish. You always had to talk over Bunny if you wanted to get your point across, and even then, it was still often lost, depending on how much she had had to drink. I didn't care. I liked telling her things like this. She was the one who *really* taught me how to love food. Of course, there were my mom and dad, but she pushed me out of my comfort zone. Like the first time we went to a Dead concert and afterward went to a bar in Nashville and she fed me oysters Rockefeller—what the hell? I didn't want to eat those slimy things, but she told me I should, so I did. And I fell in love.

August 2002. Fancy people ate at Trio. Grant's food was fun and also tasted very good but was super-duper expensive. There was this little Willy Wonka do-dad that hung on a needle, and when you set it on your tongue it tasted like a pepperoni pizza. I couldn't get over it. Pepperoni pizza. It was cheesy, and you could taste the tomatoes, fennel, sage—it was crazy. I had only ever been more inspired by writers. Like Hubert Selby, Jr., who might have been just above Grant if I'd had a running list.

Back then, when you went for a job interview it was usually after you'd seen an ad for the position in the classifieds section of the newspaper. I'd wait each Thursday for the new *Chicago Reader* to be released. I'd read through, making red checks next to potential places. But Trio I circled. I figured

even getting in the door there was an opportunity. At this point, even the name Charlie Trotter I had heard only a few times. I didn't know a lot about Trio, either, but I knew those kinds of places were way out of my reach—both eating and working there.

For me, my courage is sort of equal to my fear. There's really no middle—with anything. Rejection only taught me how to do it differently the next time. And there was that thing I learned from Tammy, who learned it from Alyssa: *What are you waiting for? Permission?* I think there was even a magnet on Tammy's fridge that said that.

I called Trio, and after a few short questions about my experience, they told me to come in that following Wednesday.

I put on the pin-striped suit I had bought on credit at Club Monaco. My hair had grown out about two inches since the last time I'd had it shaved. I had a couple of little tattoos that were easy to hide; at that time, hiding them was still necessary in order to look professional, even in the restaurant business.

Trio was in an old colonial-style building that doubled as a boutique hotel. As I stood outside, I was even more intimidated. I walked in, pulling my shoulders up to my ears, which was something I eventually learned I did without realizing it when I was a bit afraid. I asked the girl at the hotel's front desk where to go, and she pointed to a tiny corridor lined with chairs. I sat down, feeling a little claustrophobic. The walls and ceiling seemed to close in on me.

A young guy in a chef's coat, black pants, and blue apron came out and sat next to me. I reminded myself to sit up straight. I looked at my chewed nails and immediately felt

discomfort. I put my hands under my thighs. I managed to fidget anyway. I vaguely realized that he was The Chef. While a little older than me, he still seemed young—I didn't know any chefs that young. His hair was orange, and his eyes, freckles, and everything else seemed to match. He was cute, in a way—the sort of guy straight girls really like. His confidence seemed affected, learned from someone he admired. I know this to be true now because when I later became a chef, I practiced on others the confidence I learned from him.

He asked me a few questions. I can't even pretend to remember how I responded. Even in the moment I was unaware, completely blacked out. Henry Adaniya, the owner of Trio, appeared behind Grant. Henry was Hawaiian, with a squat face and kind eyes. His hair was salt-and-pepper.

"Iliana," he said.

"Yes," I responded. He pronounced my name incorrectly.

"Did I say your name right?" he asked right away.

"'Ill-ay-nuh' is the correct pronunciation, but I'm used to being called 'Ill-ee-ah-nuh,' so no worries."

He motioned for me to sit in a room across the hall. He shut the door and sat in front of me.

"What brings you to us?" he started.

A flow of honest babble poured out of my mouth, something about how I'd heard how great they were. Information wasn't as easy to collect then, not every restaurant had a website. You had to go to the library or talk with other people, both of which I had done. I told him about how my friend Natalie had acted like a fangirl when he had come into the restaurant where we worked, a queer place called Tomboy. She had said to me all swoony, "The owner of Trio is here!" I

had asked her what Trio was, and she had told me a bit about tasting menus and how much it cost. Most of it was over my head, but I had had the sense it was important.

I made him laugh a couple times, like when I said, "I want my own restaurant someday." He chortled and said it was something I shouldn't do.

I went back the following Sunday for a stage, which made me really excited. The food was immaculate and often abstract, like art. I'd never seen anything like it. I wanted the job, badly. The servers were so serious about all of the details, especially the wine, almost to a fault; it seemed pretentious. As I left that night, assuming the worst but hoping for the best, I was told Henry would be in the following Tuesday and would give me a call.

I remember I skipped school that day and nestled with my homework on the kitchen floor, just below the wall-mounted telephone. I was writing a parody of Gogol's "The Nose"—of course, my story was about a vagina and the terrible realization that occurred when it was about to get waxed. I wrote, *Why should she look that way, and for whom, when she already had such a beautiful fluffy coat to wear?* Patience is not one of my virtues. I was told Henry arrived at two each day. At 2:05, I picked up the phone and dialed.

He asked me what I thought, and I told him how impressed I was, with everything really, even down to how the servers changed the silverware between each course. (When I think back on this, I still laugh. My lack of knowledge, my innocence.)

From his voice, I sensed amusement. He told me he didn't think I was ready for a service job but that I could

be the "manager of guest relations" since that position was opening up. In short, that meant "hostess." The pay was twelve dollars an hour. Like an adult, I asked if I could think about it for the next twenty-four hours.

The decrease in pay was really not appealing. As a server, I was sometimes making about one hundred dollars a night, sometimes more. About two weeks after I walked out of Mimi's, I walked into Tomboy, also on Clark Street. It was owned by a lesbian—that place my mom took me. I think she thought it'd be good for me.

It *was* good for me. There were a lot of queer people working there, and at the time, Andersonville was still primarily a lesbian neighborhood. I didn't feel like so much of an outsider because of my sexuality. There was a community of people like me, and they had very normal, purposeful lives like other people in the world. This was comforting, even though I didn't feel near normal at all. On the second night I worked at Tomboy, I hadn't even slept the day before. I had gone to Indiana to hang out with Kate and done coke all night, blowing all the money I'd made from my first real shift. This was $140—more than I could put together in a single week at that time. So of course I went out and blew it all on booze and blow.

On my second night, I made $180. I put it in my pocket and knew this was special 'cause I had never made that much in a single day, other than when I was robbing the gas station I worked at for a while. That's a story for another time.

A full twenty-four hours later, I dialed Henry and said, "I'd be a fool not to work for you. I'll take whatever you've got."

So there I was, a hostess. It wasn't long, though, before

I became a server. We were in a staff meeting. I sat at attention, chakras aligned, next to the window, which overlooked a small garden. We reviewed the dishes and the wines that went along with them. There was a skate wing dish decorated with thin packets of mango filled with a popcorn puree. Joe Catterson, our wine director, asked what wine paired with the dish. Our fanciest, most pretentious guy, with coiffed hair and pointed eyebrows and a face full of white-boy freckles, raised his hand, and what he spat out was beyond me—all I could think about was his hair and manicured nails, his being so white-collar, white-bread white.

My hand went up too, though. I knew this answer. "Marsanne," I said when called upon, "from the Rhône."

One of the friends I had made, Scott, who was not a fan of Super White Guy either, fist pumped and said, "*That's* my girl."

Joe and Henry laughed. Later, Henry pulled me aside. Before then, he'd mostly been pulling me aside to tell me things like how to walk more precisely through a dining room, with grace and dignity. He said I swayed too much when I walked, like a cowboy. He didn't mean it as a compliment. But that day, he offered me a job as back waiter, to start as soon as we trained a new host.

Before long, I actually felt smart working at Trio. We used vegetables that I was familiar with when many of the boys in the kitchen weren't, even if they'd gone to the Culinary Institute of America or whatever. I knew why apple cider was different from apple juice. I knew when strawberries and raspberries were ripest. I knew that the yellow flowers were from zucchini by their taste. I knew sunchokes grew on the side of the road. I knew which month corn was

still tender enough to eat the whole piece, cob and all. I knew what morels and hen of the woods mushrooms were, and I knew how to find them.

The boys in the kitchen—and they were all boys—liked to talk to me because I could tell them about these things. I could talk for hours about the garden I'd flowered in. Especially when I was jacked up on coke. How the sun felt on my head and arms as I ate warm, furry raspberries. The way a tomato tastes when it's ripe from the vine, its insides warm, acidic, and sweet. How to clean pole beans and remove the fibrous spine. How to differentiate cucumber from watermelon flowers by their taste. What the three sisters are and why you grew them together. Which bugs are good for the garden and which ones aren't. The way my mom lightly breaded zucchini before it ever made it to the fridge and shallow fried it in butter. The way we dried out sunflowers for their seeds right on our back porch. How we put peppers over the fire, removed their skin, and canned them in tomato juice, olive oil, and garlic.

I told them what it smelled like when my dad sliced a deer's neck to drain the blood and pulled the fur from the length of its body. Or how you had to pour boiling water over a pig carcass to remove the tiny hairs.

It's funny, now, long after I first realized I'd been living and breathing food and cooking my entire life, to think of the people who have been resentful or jealous that I'd taught myself and didn't come up through restaurants the traditional way.

Already, Grant was a star. You could feel it standing next to him. As quiet and serious as he was, his energy was loud.

You wanted to be like him—at least, I did. By this time, I'd flunked out of engineering school and with the encouragement of Tammy, decided to study fiction writing at Columbia College. I wanted to be as passionate about writing as Grant was about food. I wanted to grow up and feel like I possessed that same amount of passion.

Trio was the beginning of the end, in a way. Once I'd worked for people like Henry, Grant, and Joe, I compared it to everything else. Then when nothing compared, I had to create it for myself. It was the same with Michael and Nathan, who opened Schwa a few years later.

Chapter 11
Death

NOVEMBER 5, 2002, WAS ELECTION DAY. CHLOE HAD been back for about five months. We had broken up for a while, and she had moved down to Florida with her parents, who still cursed my existence. Later, when Chloe's dad died of cancer, I felt bad for her. I remembered all the times she'd stolen money from his wallet so we could buy booze and fancy dinners, or baguettes and roasted garlic from a French restaurant in Miller Beach. I remember him hiding, smoking cigarettes underneath their back porch.

Once, though, when I called, he said, "You're a disgusting degenerate, and you can't talk with her because she's at her boyfriend's house. Why don't you disappear from our lives? Why do you think we left Indiana?" I mean, I couldn't have been the sole reason for their moving to Florida. They were in their fifties, for Christ's sake, and retiring. C'mon.

Disgusting degenerate.

Chloe and I had broken up a bunch of times by then, and it usually happened after some sort of drunken insanity. Once, the previous summer, she woke me up from a blackout and I threw a three-foot cast-iron candleholder. Maybe it was at Chloe, maybe it was at the wall. I'm not sure. But I do remember I was naked, and she had a bit of my hair in her fist at the back of my head when she said, "Wake up, you little bitch." I wasn't little. I was bigger than her, by at least five inches and twenty pounds.

I don't know if I had been raging before I blacked out, but if so, I was immediately right back in it. I flew out of bed like a character in a street-fighting video game—arching my back, with one leg out and the other tucked under, throwing my weight forward as I flew through the air and landed with both feet on the ground. We chased each other around the apartment, not really sure who was chasing whom. She left with a little backpack full of clothes slung over her shoulder. I ran after her, still naked.

By the time she made it to Clark Street on this lovely midsummer evening, I had already gotten ahold of her backpack and opened it, while it was still on her back, so that the clothes began falling out. I collected what I could and put them on.

By the time I was clothed, I had lost Chloe in the mix of people. I stood on the corner of Clark and Berwyn. My contacts weren't in, and everything was blurry. I remember the top I had on was turquoise; it fit tight and cropped on me, though not on Chloe. While I couldn't quite button her pants, at least they covered my crotch, where the wiry hair was threatening to show above the zipper. The pants only

came down to the base of my calves. If anyone saw me and didn't know I had just been naked, chasing my girlfriend down the street, I might have looked strange. Or maybe just like a drunk.

Reza's, the Mediterranean restaurant across the way, was very busy. Their façade opened to the street, and the restaurant sprawled out onto a patio. I heard someone calling my name. While I couldn't really see, I recognized the Texas accent and could make out an arm waving back and forth. It was a woman I'd worked with at Tomboy. I teetered on my feet, feeling and maybe looking like some sort of fisherman out of water. I had slept with this woman once, when Chloe and I were broken up, but then had called everything off when Chloe came back. I thought about going over to talk to her. I knew I'd feel comforted. At that moment, I didn't even know exactly what kind of fight I'd just been in. I was inclined to drink more. Though I had this feeling that drinking anything else that day might lead to jail—something worse than just another blackout.

Even when my drinking was at its worst, it mostly got out of control in the form of binges. The only reason I could maintain any kind of relationship with Chloe, go to school, or work was because I wasn't drinking every day. I'd have as many as four good days in between binges where I could be myself. I liked to think I was mostly a sort of sweet, generous, and creative person.

That morning of the election was shortly after that night I'd done coke with Michael and Nathan. We had wanted to

party more and weren't that far from my apartment, so we stumbled up there around three. By the time I had my key in the door, Chloe had swung it open and it hit the plaster wall, reverberating.

Her wide eyebrows formed a dramatic V across her forehead. She wanted them gone and emphasized it by jerking me into the apartment and slamming the door in their faces. She yelled, "Go the fuck home!" She pushed me onto the couch and stormed off to the bedroom. After a bit of teeth gnashing and hating myself, I fell asleep.

My memories of the fifth are like a Salvador Dali painting—one moment melting into the next: there's me walking with Chloe, pulling my peacoat tight around myself and jamming my hands into its pockets, thinking we should vote but not sure how. There's me on Church Street in Evanston, waiting for a tow truck. They were going to tow my motorcycle, which was stiff from the cold the night before. They would take it somewhere to get it looked at. As the morning unfolded, the wind became stronger and colder. I stood in the doorway of a brick building to shelter myself while I waited. I buttoned my coat up to the top, yanking the collar up and pulling a beanie far down over my ears, then walked the rest of the way to work.

There's me at work around five, just before service started, when the phone rang. Our manager came out into the dining room and said, "Iliana, your sister is on the phone." It wasn't uncommon for someone to call you at work—there weren't many cell phones at the time. At least, I didn't have one, and hardly any people I knew had one. My first thought was that my father was dead. I don't know why; I guess

because he was a little overweight and had always seemed much older than he was. He was only sixty-two, but back then, that seemed old.

My sister Nina was on the phone. "Lanie," she wailed, "Bunny died. Get to Mom's house now. *Bunny is dead.*"

I hung up the phone. I might have whispered *"OK"* before I hung up, but I don't remember. The phone was in the kitchen, and I could feel Grant side-eye me, but my conversation hadn't been long. I ran to the front and told my manager, "My sister died, I have to go."

"Get out of here," he said.

The worst part is that Elizabeth died in jail. My mom told me this when I stood in the threshold of her apartment, before I could even get inside.

I remember clearly the house where Bunny lived in Saint Pete Beach, Florida. It was a tiny ranch house with a gravel yard. Palm trees everywhere. The last time I was there, we shucked oysters with a screwdriver in her backyard, underneath the palms.

The last time I saw her, we fought. She was drunk. I was drunk. I don't even know what it was about. I remember her telling me that she was so disappointed in me because she was the one who had taken care of me. The next morning, I found her in the garage. She was dressed for work, wearing a white button shirt and black slacks. She was drinking a beer. I told her I was sorry, and she said it was fine.

She always thought of me as her own.

There are several stories about how she died, some of

which came from the jail. The women—the inmates, not the police—called Ed, her husband at the time, from the jail. They said she was blue, having a seizure, and writhing on the cement floor. They said that she had been calling for her meds but that no one responded. That by the time they got to her, she was already dead. That they tried to perform CPR, but it didn't work. That they shocked her, but it didn't get her heart started again.

About seven years later, a woman left a message in my email inbox. She said she had decided to look me up online after looking at Elizabeth's obituary, which she said she had saved 'cause they had planned to party together after they got out. She said she had spent a full night with Elizabeth in jail, and they'd had a really good time talking. She had been Bunny's cellmate and saw the whole thing go down. She said the jail killed her—the people who ran it were responsible.

Ed had seen her earlier that day in court. He was the one who had called the police the previous night. He had promised her several nights before that if she ever hit him again, he'd call the cops on her. When she punched him in the jaw that evening, he dialed 911. In Florida, when you make a 911 call and report domestic violence, the cops always show up. So the next day, after they took her to jail, Ed had to appear in court. He didn't press charges, obviously. He saw her late that morning in court, right before she died. He said she had seemed fine. The night they arrested her he had tried to give the police her medicine, but they wouldn't take it. The cop car's red lights were flashing on every wall inside the house. They had to take someone—the cops had emphasized they

had to take one or the other of them. Ed had argued with her, saying he would go instead of her.

My nieces watched from the crack in their bedroom door. Ed fumbled with the medications, shoving them on the police. They said they had their own pharmacists at the jail. He said they wrote down the prescriptions.

She was taken out of the house with her hands behind her back. He didn't think that the next afternoon, the same police officers who took her in would be ringing his doorbell with her clothes folded in a neat little pile. They held her clothes up before them, their heads slightly bowed. My nieces were in the background, plenty old enough to understand what was happening; Alexandra was eight, and Kristina turned twelve that exact day. Both wailed at the top of their lungs.

When my mom told me, I thought of my nieces. I could feel their pain—I felt like I was dying too. I fell into my mother's apartment, catching myself with my hands. It was agonizing. I really thought death, at that moment, would be better than life without Bunny. My mom said she believed my sister's dying thoughts had been about her babies, what would happen to her babies.

Bunny was an alcoholic. Everyone knew it. She didn't, though—or maybe she just accepted it. But that's what killed her, even though the coroner's report said that 95 percent of her coronary artery was blocked and she'd had a stroke.

You could also blame it on the warden for ignoring her calls and pleas, like her cellmate said, or maybe on the psychiatrist for prescribing her meds when they should have been prescribing rehab or AA. Or you could blame Ed for

calling the cops in the first place. My dad will later mull over all these scenarios, obsessively—he will blame every single person and thing.

I still sometimes blame myself. By then I had also been to jail a couple of times. The thought of her dying in a cell is the worst thing I could imagine. I thought about that happening to me. I had no clue, not the slightest bit of light to shed on how to deal with what I was feeling. I don't think any of us did.

Not long after, a friend told me she knew it wasn't much consolation, but that it's true that it gets easier over time. I can't really pinpoint a time, though, when I stopped crying about this. Time does heal, though. You wake up in the morning and start your day. Bunny is there, the acknowledgment of death, in the ether with you. Anything can make you cry or smile, just like that—a necklace, a peony, the taste of beets, a glass breaking, the way you tap a cigarette on the table, a can of Busch beer, eating oysters, French onion soup.

The grief becomes who you are. You are one sort of person, then someone you dearly love dies, and you become another sort of person. Walking over that invisible line took me years. Dropped from the womb a second time, I was a new person, one with death in her heart. I aimed to be better. I always figured I wouldn't live past the age of thirty-nine. Now that I've made it, I remember her every day, more than once. I mean, there's Elizabeth Restaurant, and later there was even Bunny Bakery. Both tributes. Both just as much a pain as easy to love.

Chapter 12
Last Drinks

PART OF MY GETTING SOBER IS JUST 'CAUSE OF THE way my sister died. I didn't want that for myself. Painful, untimely, sad, gut-wrenching, lonely. That, and I was sick of waking up in cells or beds or other places I didn't want to be.

If Carol's Pub on Clark and Leland were still around (and I were still a drunk on the drink), it's possible my name would be scrawled on the bathroom wall. In nice red Sharpie: *Call this gal for a good time*. It wasn't out of character for me to pick someone up and, after a little dancing, bang them in the bathroom. Terrible situations, ugly tennis shoes, pants around the ankles. *What the fuck was wrong with me?* I had a knack for picking the grossest people. Sometimes it was a quick fuck, sometimes it was a hand job or a blow job. With women you'd have to have more conversation first, and with that much alcohol in you, it was never a good conversation. Therefore, it was never good sex.

Guys were easier and that came with a bit of man-handling, which isn't really ever nice. But when you hate yourself, it's easy to fuck people you hate. Carol's bartenders, bouncers, and regulars had seen me in all sorts of predicaments over the years. I assume it was they who got me into cabs headed home, rather than into the vans of strangers. Raped and murdered, then reappearing in a ditch—those were things out there waiting for me. I somehow escaped through the bathroom window on those. (Once, I really did jump from a second-story bathroom window.)

In my twenties, my sexuality had a bit of fluidity, but I'm not saying that like the cool kids say it now. It was fluid because of the heavy amounts of alcohol I guzzled. It wasn't about man/woman—it was about feeling noticed or desired. Something like that. I grew up with a black-and-white filter placed over something that isn't either of those things; gender has so many forms. But when you grow up like I did, where I did, it was black and white. I grew up wanting to be a little boy. When I realized I could still like girls while being a girl, it changed everything. I took on more masculine roles in my relationships. I opened doors, paid for dinner, brought flowers—did boy things. The few times I was with boys or men, I felt like a woman. Every once in a while, that was nice. I hated and loved that role. I had this scary side to me that was so quaintly wifey—like 1950s housewife wifey. There I was, in my twenties, shaved head and all "butch," but not to the guys who liked me. They saw something else, and for purely selfish reasons, I went for it. As if I fit in with the rest of the world.

Though I slept with men, accidentally or drunkenly

tripping and falling into bed with them, I never had a true relationship with any of them. Even if sometimes I wished I could. They weren't all terrible. And part of me was always wishing to be normal, to fit in with the straight people of the world. But nope. So I always had to sit my guy "friends" down, you understand, when the next pretty or interesting girl came along, and say, "I can't sleep with you anymore, you understand?" They understood.

When I got sober, I didn't need that behavior anymore. I didn't have that emptiness, that sense of going unnoticed. Ten years of sometimes sleeping with men ended. A lot of things ended when I got sober. Say everything was completely different and I was still a drunken slut, it would take a very secure man to sleep with me. I'm not going to explain that—you know men, you can figure it out.

Anyway, my last drink was just like the first. The only things that were different were my age, location, and what I wore. You'll hear this in AA meetings sometimes if you go to one. It's just part of our story.

June 1997. My mom was shaking me. I was on the cement steps in front of our house. I was sort of collapsed over them, like I had been thrown or something. I remembered bits and pieces but not all of the gory details. Nina and my mom carried me into the house. They offered me something to eat and I refused. I hated myself, probably in direct proportion to their concern. I had worried them the night before by not showing up when I had said I would. At this point, I might just as well have been dead. They knew how I was.

My mom called my dad in for this one. Not that it made any difference. He came over from his girlfriend's apartment, where he now lived, with his girlfriend's white, fluffy dog in his Mercury sedan with black-tinted windows. They were all talking and sounded so far away, even though they were in the same room as me. Their voices were soft and crackly, like I was on the other end of the phone line in a foreign country with a terrible connection. I agreed to go to rehab—at least, to try. In the sedan, with my mom in the front, my sister and myself in the back, it was like the old days when we'd occasionally take a family trip to Pennsylvania so my dad could support a picket line, carrying his bullhorn and wearing a "USS Sux" T-shirt.

My dad worked in the mills for a long time. People there loved him. He even became president of a union, Local 1040 in Gary, Indiana. This was when I was about ten. I remember being a proud kid for a bit, telling all my friends that my dad was the president of something. Most of our family trips were so he could do union work, fighting for fair wages, workers' rights, good insurance plans. Being back together in the car felt like we were headed to a picket line again, and if we were lucky, we'd get to see some sights from whatever part of the Rust Belt we ended up in.

But everything was different now. I felt every bit as much of an alcoholic as the image you might have of one— dirty, hung over, red sunken eyes, my hair every which way, as though I'd just come from begging for change on skid row. Once at the hospital, I met with a counselor in a small room. This would be an outpatient thing. My mom and sister had told the counselor they thought I was gay—not that I needed to be treated for it, but that the repression of it might

have been causing some of my behavior. I sat there and denied it, as if I were about to be taken to jail again. *I mean, I'm sort of a tomboy but I'm not gay*, was my response. *I don't know why they would say that.*

So I was admitted. The next morning, I drove myself there. Once in group, we had an AA meeting, sort of. There was a paid counselor, which now, of course, makes no sense to me. We sat in a circle. I was seventeen years old, thin, blonde, and wearing a tank top and cargo shorts, one already faded tattoo of a star on my arm. The circle mates were all older, all shapes and sizes, all men. This was outpatient rehab, and this was my first AA meeting. They talked about sharing feelings. They talked about God.

I had just graduated after fourteen years of wearing uniforms, going to church once or twice a week, being scolded by nuns and flirted with by priests. *Fucking. A. Christ. No fucking way.* Last thing I was going to do was give my will or my mind away to God. Or whatever the hell these people were asking me to sacrifice—my firstborn or whatever. *Fuck you.*

I stayed sober twenty-six days and was actually really proud of myself. There was no God or higher power, though—just willpower. Then, on the Fourth of July, I was at my friend Jill's house. Chloe, Jill, and Jill's grandpa, who still had a Slavic accent, were in the garage. They were drinking beer.

I had on an American flag bikini top and cutoff shorts. A girl of the American midwestern wilderness. My hair was really long and really blonde, and we were all very tan. Jill's grandpa, who was old and mean to the bone, like I imagine every Slavic grandpa to be, called us porch monkeys. We

didn't laugh. Wasn't funny then, isn't now. Wilderness or not, we were a bit more woke.

I sat on the chrome bumper of the two-toned Jeep Wagoneer in the garage. I pulled a Coors Light, all cold and shiny, little beads of water dripping down it, from the cooler. So pretty. And like nothing had happened, I just started drinking. All the days of not drinking were thrown away in a second.

I should have gone home when I was supposed to; my promise to myself had been to attend only the parade, but here I was well past all that—the parade, then Jill's garage, then the beach, then Dave's house party. Dave wasn't my friend, but I knew him. He was always pretty nice to us. He bought us liquor and tried to drink it with us. We were mean—we would always figure out a way to ditch him. He was too old.

When I pulled up in the cul-de-sac, people were still arriving, sunburnt from their Independence Day activities. The sun was already gone, the sky a little pink at the tree line beyond the house. The garage door was open, and CCR was on the radio. The neighborhood was sparse. A few fireworks cracked overhead and fizzled, the smoke blending into the clouds behind them. You could see a few stars if you could stop swaying enough. As I walked up, I could see Chloe; she was silhouetted by the lights from the garage, and this guy put his arm around her. He slowly turned his head, as he sensed I was behind them. He locked eyes with me; his face was gnarled with acne.

He said creepily, "Your girlfriend is a mad tongue-kisser."

Without hesitation, I punched him in his ugly mug. Just like that, as in any good bar fight, chaos ensued. I grabbed a

spatula from the grill and began swatting humans like flies. I accidentally punched Jill's brother when he tried to stop me. It ended with some girl with lots of long hair pouring beer in my car. The cops showed up, and the people at the party accused me of drinking and driving—there was that beer all over my car—and told them that I was a homo.

I sat in my car with the windows up. People stood in front of it, demanding I get out. The cop knocked her knuckle against my window. I cracked it.

"Are these things true?"

"Yes," I said. "Not the homo part, but I did punch a guy for saying stupid things to me."

"OK," she hesitated. She looked around. "Go home," she said.

She motioned for the small crowd in front of my car to move. Chloe's brother and his girlfriend looked at me like I'd done something really bad to them. Chloe had vanished. I found out later that she'd taken off as soon as the fighting had started. She said later that her brother had told her she was a disgusting little bitch. That's when she ran. She said she didn't want to be there to hear the name-calling. She didn't want to hear people be mean to me.

She also said she didn't want to be associated with me. Lots of those people I never saw again. I did see Dave once, though, in his pickup. I waved and he just kept driving, pretending not to see me.

January 2001. My mom sat across from me in the apartment Chloe and I shared for a bit. She looked small in a big

saucer-like chair. I sat on the futon. I rested my elbows on my knees and locked my hands between them. I was starting to look like a pool stick. Black T-shirt, black jeans, black boots, and black beanie, with a black cloud over me.

I was telling my mom about depression and anxiety, that perhaps I had them. I wasn't good at showing up to things, and when I did, I was usually tangibly hung over. I mean, I was smelly or looked unwell, or both. I was still in school. I was still working. But those things always hung by a thread.

I'll usually agree to something when I'm hung over or in trouble or feeling guilty. She said, "I know someone at work who goes to AA."

I rolled my eyes. "I tried that."

"You didn't. You stopped after less than a month. We paid all that money for you to get help, and then you quit and threw it away with one night of drinking. Look what happened. You almost became a statistic."

She was right.

So at the end of January 2001, I went to AA again. I met my mom's friend at a coffee shop on Clark Street in downtown Chicago. We sat at a small table next to the window. Snow fell. The windows fogged over. He casually asked me what was up with my drinking. I told him nothing that bad, except for my winding up in jail. He told me that wasn't normal but still laughed.

"Once you start drinking, is it hard to stop?"

"Yes."

"Can you ever just have one or two drinks?"

"Not really."

172

"Do you black out when you drink?"

"Yes."

"Does your mind race?"

"Every second."

"There's a meeting one block away from here, and it starts in ten minutes." He paused and sipped his coffee. "Want to go?"

"Yes."

The meeting was in the basement of a pretty limestone cathedral on Dearborn Street, but the basement was like every other church basement: vinyl, checkered floors and dropped ceilings, the acoustic tiles stained from years of burst pipes and leaks. I never felt right in church.

I wore a black leather motorcycle jacket zipped up tight, a black beanie, a black scarf. As we walked farther into the room, I took off my knitted mittens, the only thing I had on that wasn't black. I shoved my hands in my pockets. I sort of took my time removing my winter gear and fumbled with things so I didn't have to make eye contact. I left on my black beanie because I knew I was going to look even more out of place with no hair among these well-dressed yuppie types. When you go to an AA meeting, it's like you're naked, except it's your thoughts and feelings that are exposed. It's like you put on a costume to make everyone think you're OK—like a nice jacket, clean mittens, designer jeans, expensive shoes, a clean house, you're working toward a degree—but at AA, nothing can keep everyone from finding out that you're not. You walk into that church basement, and any semblance of being OK is gone.

I didn't see anyone there like me. I don't know what I

was looking for, maybe someone else to seem gay or sort of punk rock. They all just seemed like each other.

I sat in a folding chair. I barely looked at the lady next to me, but she still stuck her hand out to me and told me her name. I shook it.

"Cold hand," she said.

I said something like, "Warm heart, yada yada." I smiled and looked down. I was trying my hardest to seem somewhat normal, but there was no escaping things. Sober people know when you haven't been sober very long.

She said, "You're new."

I said, "I guess so. I was in outpatient once. Stayed dry for close to thirty days."

"Hmmm," she hummed. "This will be a good meeting for you. But if you don't like it, there's thousands all over the city."

At the start of the meeting, new people were asked to raise their hands. I did. I took the lead and said, with ease, "My name is Iliana. I'm an alcoholic." Some people struggle with that. I didn't. I knew.

We all listened to a girl a little older than me give a lead. That means she told her story. I didn't hear much. It was like white noise in my head, fuzzy. After the meeting, maybe because I was new, a couple of women walked over to me while I was wrapping my scarf back up around my neck and face. They asked if I wanted to go to another meeting that night. It was a Friday and rare that I was off of work, but I was. I said yeah.

I stayed sober for one week. It ended when Stephanie, a girl who liked me, asked if I wanted to go out. I sort of liked her too. She was cute, sort of punk. Mostly I remember her pink lipstick and the safety pins she wore in her clothes. She

was funny. She had tickets to see Lords of Acid at the Vic. I didn't know how to be out in public like that without drinking. Stephanie knew I was trying to stay sober. We'd hung out a couple times before, and she'd said she thought it was a good thing I wasn't drinking.

Everyone at the Vic was punk. Piercings in their faces, wearing black, torn things, studded belts or shoes, chain wallets. I fit in, like a skinny little punk boy with a girl face. I had a wallet chain, steel-toe boots, the whole deal. I'd had lots of styles over the years: my head shaved, looking punk. Or in a hippie skirt and crop top with my hair in a long braid. Or with my hair slicked into a pompadour, riding up on my motorcycle. Or in a flannel with a wavy bob, my face and body a little bloated.

When Stephanie and I got into the show, it was dark but for the stage. There was a large blow-up Satan doll, but it was all sexy and woman-shaped, with a long red tail whipping around. The girl on the stage wore a leather outfit and had long braids she flung in circles. She screamed into the microphone, "Show me your pussy! I wanna see your pussy!"

The strobe lights flickered over the crowd, and lasers vibrated over everyone's heads, making me feel like I was going to pass out or have a heart attack. Just like nothing, I walked to the bar and got a beer. I drank it before Stephanie even knew I was gone. Then I got another. I drank that too. Then I got another and walked back over to her and her friends. The lights weren't bothering me anymore. I bounced up and down with her and her friends to the music and for the most part, felt good. I had fun. I screamed along with the song, "Show me your pussy! I wanna see your pussy!"

We got back to my place at one. My old friend Kate was over with our friend Charlie. It was like that sometimes. My friends just showed up. Girls didn't always like Kate because she was pretty but that never bothered me. Girls don't like other pretty girls sometimes. I like other pretty girls, but it wasn't like that with me and Kate. Charlie was mostly her friend. Stephanie was being kind of shy, and when she realized that I was going to party more, she split. There was no way I was going to run into Kate and Charlie and not party more. So I got up on my dresser—I mean, stood on it—and began to sing for them the crazy song I had just heard. I told them about the sexy Satan doll on the stage and all the other wacky things, and we laughed our asses off.

Charlie and I went on a beer run in Kate's VW, as only fucked-up idiots would do, to the liquor store two blocks away. Walking would've been smarter, but that's not what drunk people do.

We got to a red light and there was no one on the street except a taxi in the opposite lane. We were facing south, the taxi north. We both waited, and when the light took too long, I swiftly took a left turn. Charlie and I laughed, but then red lights and sirens showed up behind us. I decided there was no way in hell I was going to let us get arrested. I threw my arm across Charlie's chest and told him to hold on tight. I pressed my foot on the gas and sped down Foster Avenue. Right before Glenwood Avenue, I swung north into an alley.

There were no speed bumps in the alleys back then, and I drove as fast as I could, zig-zagging up and down streets and alleys until I was sure I'd lost them. I wrenched the wheel back and forth, making as many turns as I could. Charlie

and I turned around and looked out the back window, our eyes peeled. We skidded and slid around corners. One side of the car pinged off a garbage can, sending it flying. The red lights faded away. When I couldn't see them anymore and it was all dark again but for streetlights, we swung into a grocery store parking lot. We locked the doors and got out, our hearts pounding. We started walking down the road and patted each other on the back. Charlie had been scared. I was too but was almost too drunk to care. Charlie shouted for me to stop. He wanted to go back to my house.

"IF I STOP, WE ARE BOTH GOING TO JAIL. NO!" I yelled.

We walked to Simon's. I pulled a crumpled five from my pocket and ordered us two Schlitzes each. I exchanged a dollar for quarters for the jukebox. We played "Ring of Fire." Charlie kept reliving the chase. I kept reminding him it was a good thing we weren't in jail. We left the last two quarters on the bar.

When we walked back into the night, into that early-morning silence, we were the loudest thing on the street. The orange-black Chicago sky broke open and dumped rain on our heads, and we ran back to my apartment.

December 25, 2009. I was in my friend's car. We were driving back from my family's Christmas celebration in Indiana. All I could think about were the things I'd heard over the years in AA, that I'd never have to feel this way again.

Helen was my girlfriend. The night I met her, at the place where I tended bar, I thought she looked like an

actress. Her hair was long and black. Her coat was crisp. Her glasses looked expensive. She had on a diamond ring and diamond earrings. Her boots where nice. She was just all around very put together. I watched her all night. She seemed confident.

I wanted to be like that but never really could. I couldn't talk with confidence unless I had a few bottles of beer in me. I was shy. I always felt nervous. I was good at being a bartender, though. I knew wine from the years at Trio. I knew beer 'cause I drank lots of it. I knew classic cocktails from all the late nights I'd spent at Viet Brasserie reading the cocktail handbook. I could carelessly flirt with people—I knew how to do that, and it was good for tips. Lots of girls noticed me there. Especially after they started drinking, they'd feel more comfortable talking to me and would ask me out. But I didn't go out with many of them.

I wanted to talk to this woman, but she didn't seem to notice me. She wouldn't even hold eye contact for longer than it took to request a glass of white wine. When I finally built up the courage to ask her if she'd like to go out sometime, she was already handing me her card to pay. I suppose I could have asked her then, but . . . I looked at her name on her card. Helen Richards.

I didn't go out that night or even drink, that I recall. Probably hung over from the night before. The next morning, she was the first thing I thought about after I opened my eyes. I went straight to find her. After a few social media searches, I found her.

I sent her a message: "Hey. I think you are really beautiful. I was your bartender last night. By the time I had built

up the courage to ask you out, you were gone. I'd like to take you out. Sorry if this seems creepy, but I looked at your name on your credit card."

No more than a few minutes passed before I got a response back: "My, how lovely. I'd like that." *Holy smokes.* My heart jumped in my throat.

My mom and I had been sharing an apartment since 2007. In the summer of 2009, my friend John moved in with us. All sorts of strays came our way. John and his girlfriend had broken up in a bad way and he had nowhere else to go, and he didn't want to head back to Iowa.

John and I had met while working at Alinea. When I first met him, I admired his height and beauty. His eyebrows spanned the width of his geometric face. We spent time together, as friends at first, and as we drank, which we both did very well, things began to happen. One night we'd ended up in bed together. Over the next year, John and I slept together on and off, but when I met a woman I liked, or he did, we would stop. It was all about drinking for us. When we hung out, we drank. If we woke up together, we drank. If we did anything, we drank. By the time he moved in, we were more or less friends; we'd had so many women come between us that being anything more was weird. John has always remained attractive to me—he's smart and funny too. I even thought at one point that maybe I could choose the road of least resistance—not actually be straight but maybe wear it like an outfit. But I knew deep down, I couldn't change that way.

After a series of texts back and forth, Helen and I decided she would come over for dinner. My mom was home

that evening. John was off work, hanging out with Justin, an old acquaintance from Alinea. This was in September and it was still very nice and warm. I spent most of the day playing out the evening in my mind. John and I waited for Helen on the back porch. We'd already had a couple of beers and opened a bottle of wine. I felt able to control my drinking a little, as I usually could at the beginning of any relationship. John had a guitar and was strumming little tunes. Our back porch overlooked the garden I liked to tend; I planned to serve tomatoes from that garden as part of our dinner. It faced west, and the sun was just showing above the rooftops when Helen showed up in the alley.

"Hey," I said, surprised and trying to contain my excitement.

"I didn't have a signal out front to text you."

"I'll be right down."

I looked at John for approval. He smiled and nodded. He approved.

She came up and I gave her a glass of wine. We sat on the porch for a while, as I had already prepared most of the dinner; I only needed to assemble. We smiled a lot. She gently touched my arm a few times to make it clear we were where we needed to be.

I had slow-roasted rib eye in butter. I had blended fresh herbs from our garden with olive oil and lemon juice. I had seared endives in our cast iron until they were golden brown and sliced fresh tomatoes coated with salt and vinegar. We drank more wine. Justin arrived in the middle of dinner with a few nice German wines. Helen recognized Justin from Alinea and connected the dots—we were all accomplished

in the wine and food worlds. Otherwise I might have been a little less interesting to her, I feared. My mom sat down with us. It felt serendipitous. I liked to cook for girls, if I liked them. I didn't even mind cooking for John. I made him breakfast in the middle of the night. A lot.

After dinner, we were not ready for the night to end, so we went to Edgewater Lounge, which had live bluegrass on Tuesdays. The band wasn't great, but the bar was close by, it was fun, and it had good beers. The banjo provided background music when Helen and I escaped from John and Justin, who had been talking over each other, trying to be the smartest and funniest, showing off. We went to the back of the building and sat on the bumper of my pickup truck. I had driven there, still maintaining my dignity. I complimented her and she complimented me back, and later I walked her the five blocks to where she lived; we had decided together that walking would be better than driving. When we got close to her house, she grabbed me by my shoulders, pushed me into a gangway, and kissed me. From the moment she came up to my porch that night, I knew I was going to fall in love with her, and I did.

Helen was about to move, and she also traveled a lot for work. Most of my memories of our relationship are of my pining for her while she was away, waiting for her return, and then counting the too-few days until she'd be gone again. I wasn't able to contain my drinking for very long after we got together, but the truth is it had already been pretty bad. I tried to control myself, but anytime I had a drink, blacking out was more and more inevitable. Helen always reminded me the next day of the things I'd said or

done, as would John or Justin, if we'd seen them. On one particular morning, Justin told me that the night before, I'd vomited a little on myself while sitting on Helen's lap. The worst.

For some reason, she stuck around. Helen wasn't an alcoholic by any means, but she'd had alcoholics close to her throughout most of her life. So when she saw me drink the way they drank, she went into savior mode. I really wanted to maintain a relationship with her. I thought it could save me a little. I knew that wasn't how it worked, but I hoped, maybe . . .

But I couldn't keep sober for her. I kept pushing the limits, and she kept waking up next to me. We lasted until about December before she finally told me I needed to stop drinking so much around her. We were on her living room floor at the time. Somehow, we had made it through the evening without any drinks. She lay on top of me, her hair shadowing my face. I was thinking I was pretty lucky. She was smart, beautiful, and kind.

"You can't get drunk around me anymore like you do," she said.

My heart sank a little. My initial reaction was that I had let her down. Then I felt bad because I had been telling myself it was working—that I could be with this woman and drink however I wanted. I felt exposed. She was telling me, though, in a very gentle way, that it wasn't working. Not for her. I didn't say anything in response.

"I'm not saying you *can't* drink. You can do whatever you want. I *am* saying you can't get drunk anymore around me, or I can't be around."

"OK," I said, defeated. I was getting used to hearing this. I wanted, very deep down, to stop.

A few days before Christmas, Helen was going to Louisville to spend time with her family. She'd be gone for about six days. We planned a date. That evening, my niece Kristina, who was twenty, was visiting, and I had been out Christmas shopping all afternoon. I brought a pizza home for her and my mom. I set the pizza on the counter, went into the refrigerator, and took out a beer. I knew I was asking for trouble. By this time in my life, it took very little for me to get drunk. Sometimes only one or two drinks could kick in the alcohol still lingering in my system from the night before. I was having a lot of trouble sobering up in between days that I drank.

I opened the beer and drank it down as fast as I could. Before she knew how much I drank, Helen had bought me a nice bottle of scotch. It was a cute gesture, but she did sort of side-eye me when I immediately opened it and put some in a flask so I could take it to work. John and I were working together then at a place called Table Fifty-Two, and I was also making pierogi for farmers markets and some stores around the city.

I drank the beer fast because I was afraid to see Helen while I was sober. I was so afraid of doing or saying the wrong thing, and when I was buzzed, all that went away. I felt more confident, even though she disliked it. I cared less. I had already told her, on some night back in October, that I loved her. I was drunk, of course, but it still happened. Or so she told me, because I didn't remember. The next day, she had asked me if I remembered anything from the night before. Of course I didn't. Turns out I was whispering a Neko Case song to her in bed, like, "I love you. I love you. I love

you. This tornado loves you. What will make you believe me?" And then I passed out.

She had replied, which I also didn't remember, that she believed me and that she loved me too.

The buzzer to our front door rang. I put the last piece of tape around the Frosty the Snowman paper wrapping the cowboy boots I'd gotten for her. She came in. I could tell she was assessing me, and I knew my face betrayed that I'd been drinking. But I was coherent and happy and excited. I grabbed her by the hand and led her to my room. I kissed her. I gave her the box.

"I thought we weren't doing presents."

"Yeah, yeah, I know. But, well, I always say things I don't mean."

She smiled. "Well, good, 'cause I have something for you too."

We took a cab to the restaurant. Guys I used to know treated us like queens, taking us to the best table and sending out lots of dishes we didn't order. I ordered a half bottle of white wine and a full bottle of red. She always let me order the wine. After dinner, we had amaro and coffee. I still remember the meal—lamb-neck nachos, charred octopus, sea bass, and mushrooms. We took a cab to her house that evening, and the next morning, she took me home and headed down south.

John and I worked together on December 23, and after our shift, we went out with coworkers and tied it on. I knew it wasn't a good idea—by then, I rarely went out anymore outside of my neighborhood, for fear of what could happen. John had moved out and had a new roommate, one of our

managers. Lots of whiskey left me unable to drive. The next day, I woke up in John's bed. Nothing had happened, but I was in a pretty bad way and tried to collect myself. He was already gone, headed back to Iowa, and had left me a note telling me Merry Christmas and he loved me and was happy I was in his life.

I talked with Helen for a while as I lay there slowly putting the globby pieces of my brain back in my skull. She was warm in Louisville. I told her of my reckless night and explained I was still a little drunk. She could tell, she said, but I was making her laugh, and that was all I cared about at the moment. I was telling her nonsensical stories about our unborn children and the mileage on her car. Gunning off about this and that. Making a joke that made no sense to anyone other than us.

When I finally got up, I went to Whole Foods to get a few dry goods for making pierogi, and also beer because somehow, I was going to need to get through the rest of the day. As I was turning into the parking lot, I hit a pole.

I have no idea what happened. I might have blacked out for a split second while turning. It was crazy. It was icy, maybe I had slid or something. All I could think was how happy I was that no one was between my truck and that pole—especially considering I had gone over a sidewalk to hit it.

I was also so happy that I had missed any traffic, because I had had to cross two lanes to get there.

I called my insurance company to get the truck towed. I told the parking lot attendant a tow truck was on the way, then walked into Whole Foods and bought my beer and my groceries. I told the manager on duty about my truck

and that I must have slid on the ice, which could have been true even though it wasn't. Everyone said it would be fine. I went to the coffee shop next door to get out of the way before any cops showed up and began poking around. I knew I still smelled like alcohol. There was no way I didn't. I hadn't showered that day or the night before.

I called Helen. She sounded disappointed, like maybe she thought I'd had more to drink or that something wasn't adding up somehow. She listened, though. I called my mom, who came and picked me up. She railed at me for smelling like alcohol. She refused to drive me to Indiana with her for dinner for the holiday, and now I didn't have the truck to drive down there the next day myself, so I was sort of screwed. When my mom dropped me off at home, she told me I was worthless and that I had better not drink her beer. Yeah, right.

Fortunately, my friend Darko was going to borrow a car from his friend Antonia, who liked me, so we'd have transportation, he reassured me. The two of them came over that evening.

I got drunk. We went to a party together, and when we got home, I could barely walk up the stairs. There I was, again, with a tall, buff, blonde man carrying me upstairs to put me to bed, just like the first time I got drunk. He tucked me in. The next morning was like I'd split my head on the cement. Again.

Darko and I went to my sister Kelley's house and spent the day with my family. I knew my mom had told everyone what happened, and I felt stupid and ashamed. Again.

When we drove back to Chicago that night, we were on

the Dan Ryan Expressway and I just kept remembering this saying I had heard over the years in AA, that I'd never have to feel this way again.

Of course, I had crashed my truck, but it wasn't like anything *extremely* bad had happened. That was the fourth car I'd crashed while drunk over the years. I hadn't injured anyone too badly. No deaths. I wasn't back in jail. I kept hearing it, though: *I'd never have to feel this way again.* I suddenly realized everything was on the line. Work was going OK. I was dating a beautiful, smart woman whom I loved. My family was still supportive of me, if disappointed. People like Darko were still willing to bail me out of my mistakes. I understood, though, that it wasn't going to be much longer before it was all gone. It was like I could read it in everyone's eyes.

The day after Christmas was a Saturday. For years, there were meetings at a church in my neighborhood on Saturday mornings at 10 a.m. I knew 'cause every once in a while, since that first meeting I went to in the city, I'd drop in when I needed to put some sober time together. I woke up, finally not hung over, and went to the meeting.

It had been a little over a year and a half since I had set foot there, but I recognized a lot of the people. I took a spot at the back. Standing room only, so I held up the wall.

The meeting started and the chairperson asked, "Is there anyone here with less than thirty days?"

I put up my hand. "Hi. My name is Iliana, I'm an alcoholic, and I have twenty-four hours."

That was the last time.

Part
Three

Chapter 13
Becoming the Boss Lady

GIRL BOSS: I THOUGHT ABOUT GETTING THE LETTERS tattooed across my knuckles. Instead, I got Elizabeth's signature. As the sting of the needle grazed my chest, I knew for sure that day that I'd name my first restaurant after her. I made a plan.

Late one night, I looked up how to start a small business. Maybe I'd need to talk to someone. The City of Chicago has a help center. I set an appointment. When the day arrived, I dressed up in a suit with a tie and everything. I'd learned how to make pretty knots by watching the boys at work in pre-shift. I did that, put on a bit of makeup, and went down to meet with a counselor. There I was, sitting on my hands again. The building was chilly, so I didn't take off my jacket. These men didn't get to see my tie.

Instead, the bald man who sat in front of me laughed when I told him my plan was to have a farmhouse, the kind

like a log cabin, maybe with some woods and a garden, and I'd make beautiful dinners on this self-sustaining property. I'd grow all my own food, can, preserve, hunt, fish, forage. He got stuck on this and challenged me on legality, food safety, and storage. *Huh?* I told him about bed-and-breakfasts I'd been to and fancy restaurants I had worked at and the farm I grew up on. I said maybe I'd just have a farm and then a restaurant in the city. We went back and forth on my ideas. Each time, I tried to fit them into his box, but he didn't care. He told me I would need more money than I could probably get. I asked him the likelihood of a bank helping me, and he said without my own money, things like what I wanted just don't happen. I left. I wasn't discouraged 'cause somehow I knew this guy couldn't hear me.

Now, officially without permission, I was going to do it, regardless of what those weird freakin' buzzards said. At the end of January 2008, I was working front of house at Alinea, and I would get home from work as late as two in the morning. I'd sit at the kitchen table. I'd unwrap my scarf, hat still on, open a beer, and study tiny gardens.

I had decided I was going to start my own little self-sustaining business. I was twenty-eight. I thought I could either go back to school to get a master's and get further in debt, or I could just open the restaurant I'd always wanted.

When I was young, I'd imagined having an old Victorian house with a restaurant on the inside, maybe a bed-and-breakfast, something like that. I'd dreamt it up a long time ago while visiting Elizabeth when she lived in Georgia: large grapevines crawling up the walls and pillars; a front porch as big as the house itself; old windows, ten feet tall, open; a little

bluegrass or fiddle music to ping along in the background, the kind that makes you shrug your shoulders along with it. I imagined candlelight along the tabletops and just beyond that, in the garden outside the windows, fireflies mimicking the flicker of the candles. I was going to do it.

I would get home at two and then read piles of books on all things gardening and food. I began sprouting sunflowers, corn, and peas in my pantry. I grew mushrooms in the bathroom. I began to culture buttermilk and cream and made my own butter. I added rennet to milk and cream, tied it all up in cheesecloth, and made cheese. Everywhere you went in my apartment there was a project.

Mom wasn't excited about the milk curdling in the pantry or the mushrooms growing in the shower, but she was glad I wasn't stumbling in drunk out of my goddamned mind every night. I was still drinking, of course. But this other passion, to pursue my ideas, was beginning to change me. I was able to direct my thinking more in a way that helped me avoid my other obsessions. I was only drinking a few beers a night. I was also doing better at my actual job. When I didn't drink like an idiot, I was learning, I was sort of better at everything.

Summer 2008. I got a stall at a farmers market in Crown Point, Indiana. It was easier there than in Chicago—the health department didn't need nearly as much paperwork. I had to be there and be set up every Saturday morning by eight. I got up at five in the morning to make the trip. Sometimes I would have only returned home from work a few hours before. I packed up my little Ford Ranger with a tent,

two tables, some kitschy tablecloths, and all of my things: strawberry preserves, a few bundles of fresh beets, two-ounce bags of sunflower sprouts, corn shoots, radish sprouts. Drop biscuits, homemade butter, dried morel mushrooms my dad and I had gathered. Homemade pasta. Little bottles of buttermilk ranch dressing with the homemade buttermilk and herbs from my garden. Two heads of lettuce I'd grown and a dozen tortillas I'd made with wheat I'd sprouted. I assembled wraps with all the sprouts, ranch, and tortillas.

A few people lined up. They were mostly curious. It was sort of perfect and imperfect at once. I was really proud, even though sales were low; at first, I only made between $100 and $200 per market. Selling at the market taught me how to be concise and clear, and at that moment, I wasn't either of those so much. But from that first market, I began to build a brand. I incorporated and called it One Sister, thinking of Elizabeth, but mostly thinking I was one sister, one woman, trying to do all of this—grow, make, eat.

By summer 2009, I was signed up for several farmers markets in Chicago. One Sister was more than just a sustainable little mash-up of goods I dug out of my pantry or towel closet on Saturday mornings. The summer prior had ended with me taking all of my beets, mixing them with my homemade ricotta, and stuffing them into the dough my mother had taught me, and which she had learned from her Uncle Frank. Pierogi. I hauled those warm beet pierogi to the market, and I sautéed them in tons of butter right on the spot. As it turned out, a few places in Chicago heard about these pierogi and asked me to sell them in their stores. Then, in the middle of summer 2009, an article was

published about me and my pierogi, and I got hundreds of orders. Now I had to figure out shit like packaging—this, really, forced me to start a business. Word continued to spread, and in 2010, *Chicago* magazine called my pierogi the best in the city. *This is not a small thing*, I thought, *with all the Polish in Chicago.*

Next, I had to figure out a way to make it known that I could cook. I already knew I could basically do everything needed to operate a restaurant business. I'd been a dishwasher, salad girl, dessert girl, and line cook; I'd cooked pho, Chinese, country French, and Italian; I'd worked as a server, manager, captain, and back waiter; I'd studied wine and bused tables. I'd been a chef. I had to do this thing, though: I needed to put together my own curriculum to learn everything I'd been missing in the kitchens over the years. So when I wasn't doing my farmers markets or working as a server, I was staging in kitchens. Staging can be mutually beneficial. If you want, like in my situation, you can go in with a running list of all the things you want to learn and learn them. Or you can do all the cutting and slicing the commis don't want to do. I did both and was happy to do it. All along the way, I was teaching myself more modern techniques. I studied day and night. Once I got sober, this all became much easier. But really, I was still a little naïve.

Every once in a while, if I'd saved enough money, I'd work in a kitchen again. I was pretty good and would quickly gain a management position as either sous chef or head chef. I was creative, which my bosses liked; it wasn't something I

was taught, but something I tapped. I was still drinking a lot, though. And I had little idea how to manage people properly. What I had mostly seen and learned regarding management, even at places like Trio and Alinea, was that as far as the kitchen goes, if you wanted something done your way, you yelled. You made yourself so scary that employees would fall in line and do what you were saying. I had a hard time with this. And when you're a woman and you yell, it doesn't have the same effect as the guys yelling. They were like army sergeants. I was just a "crazy bitch."

I was the head chef at a little Swedish restaurant on the North Side for a bit. Sometimes I was so hung over I had to lean against the kitchen wall as I prepped so I wouldn't lose my balance. It was just my second position as head chef, and I still didn't really know jack shit about running a kitchen. What I could do, though, was cook pretty well. While I still had much to learn, I had a good imagination and I could make the food look pretty.

I had been the chef there for about five months when an older lady came in with her son. She ordered the pork chop and carrots. I'll never forget this 'cause it's such an emblem of my alcoholism. She asked for her carrots to be cooked soft. OK. So I cooked them a little extra. They were sent back, so I cooked them more.

When they came back a third time, I looked at the server, hit the lowboy refrigerator with my tongs, and said, "How about this—I'll eat those fucking carrots, then I'll shit them out, and then serve them again. Will that be soft enough?"

The lady's son overheard and came to the kitchen window. "I heard what you said," he told me.

I was still at the stove. Without turning to him, I said, "If she can eat that pork chop, she can eat those fucking carrots."

He said a few more things, and after each remark, my reply did not change: "If she can eat that pork chop, she can eat those fucking carrots."

My boss and his wife were Swedish. They had five blonde children and were very nice people. When Mr. Anderson looked in my eyes and asked for my resignation, I gave it immediately. I knew this wasn't going to slide. Little did I know that when I was the boss, I was going to face these same sorts of situations, with these same sorts of chefs. Instant karma's gonna get you. (I didn't say that, John Lennon did.) OK, so maybe sometimes I was a crazy bitch.

I did a whole bunch of other things. There were about three good years of drinking, staging, serving, farmers markets, and pierogi. I was in and out of a couple quick relationships. In some odd way, I was going through a kind of spiritual experience without knowing it. I was changing the course of my entire life. I can see it now, but back then I was surprising myself, over and over.

May 2010. I set up a restaurant in my house. I was a server at Table Fifty-Two, where I'd heard Art Smith say the phrase "underground restaurant." I went home that night and did research. I could do this. I had already incorporated myself. I was learning bookkeeping. I'd made a little name, had a few press contacts, taught myself how to do social media and PR. There was no reason I shouldn't open a restaurant in my house.

I had about $3,000 saved up, more money than I'd ever had at once. I'd sold my pierogi to lots of drunk people at an event called Dark Lord Day, held every year at my favorite brewery, Three Floyds. I was then only four months sober. It was scary, but I muscled through it, emerging with a few extra wrinkles and a lot more gray hair.

After being in and around kitchens like those at Alinea, L20, Schwa, and others almost as fancy, I had to be very careful about what equipment I could and could not buy. I remembered things like watching Grant cook sous vide in the Trio kitchen back in 2002 by wrapping pork very tightly in plastic wrap and cooking it in a big pot of water with a thermometer, occasionally dropping ice cubes into the pot to regulate the temperature. I could do that. I didn't need the fancy stuff. But those fancy places—even Schwa—all had a Pacojet, a machine that will take any frozen substance and essentially make it beautiful and smooth. In response, I began to study how different stabilizers worked in ice cream—or in anything, for that matter. I had learned how to use them during my stages, but I didn't necessarily know how they worked. When I was in school all those years, I had been pretty good at chemistry and mathematics, and I was always fascinated by how things worked in conjunction with one another to produce a result. Between my experience and my aptitude for science, I had everything I needed.

I'd do things like go to the store and find different kinds of ice cream that had textures I liked, delving deep into the ingredients on their labels and taking notes of all the stabilizers. Were you pissed at that woman turning all the ice cream around, standing half in the freezer and half in the

aisle, writing on her hand as she scanned the labels? Yeah, that was me.

Then I would experiment with the stabilizers. This kind of research and experimentation became the basis of my method—not just with ice cream but with almost everything. It was slow and laborious but worth it. I was obsessed with almost everything I could cook. I did the same with baking biscuits or bread or whatever. Study and practice. My underground dinners basically became the laboratory part of my self-education.

When I look back at those first dinners, I feel a little embarrassed. Though I'm still proud of the cornbread cookies that I sandwiched around oyster ice cream, dotting the tops with a pink peppercorn fluid gel. I served it on a frozen piece of glass-block window. And of the potato and truffle pierogi with homemade mascarpone. Oh, and the pretty little crispy nests of spaghetti squash that I put in twigs stuck in wheatgrass I grew. The dry-aged rib eye with a dark demi-glace, red wine with peppercorn marshmallows, and bull blood–seasoned barley risotto.

In addition to Helen and my sponsor, among the guests at my very first dinner were a handful of people from the press who had written before about my pierogi. I had asked them if they'd be interested in writing about my underground dinners. They were interested. And after they wrote about them, I was all booked up for the rest of the summer. I served twelve guests a night, Friday and Saturday, back-to-back, every other weekend. People paid a hundred dollars per person and brought their own bottles of wine. Some of my amazing new AA friends helped; they'd end up becoming

my best friends. One would be a server and the other a dishwasher, and I did the rest—all the prep, all the cooking. I learned to manage food costs, plan accordingly, and handle guest relations. I learned how to take photos to promote myself, and I slowly built my little business.

The dinners were fun. I started to get recognition, not least because I foraged for a lot of the ingredients, which I just saw as staying true to my roots. I cooked what I knew. I canned, pickled, and preserved as many things as I could from my garden. It was charming, even if it wasn't all very good. I was playing with ingredients and playing with stories. Everything I did had a story. I was escaping and letting people get to know me all at once. I was doing things that were all buzzwords at the time, like farm to table, and foraging, and organic, and sustainable. Thing is, I'd learned to do those things before they were popular hashtags. In writing class we were once told, and I'm paraphrasing, "You don't have to go any further than your own backyard to write a good story." The same is true for cooking.

Right from the start, I had a few investment offers. While these were not always real, they were all worth chasing. At the time, I was pushing as hard as I could. Each time I thought I was ready, a potential investment would fall through, and I'd realize how not ready I actually was. I cannot understate, though, how doing everything myself made for such an immense learning experience. Along the way, I taught myself many things about cooking that I don't think I could have ever learned in school. I was well-rounded. There was still a lot more, however, I had yet to learn. Things no one can teach you.

Chapter 14
Yes, Chef

"I DRY-AGED THIS SQUAB FOR A FEW WEEKS."

I hold it up and show the guests sitting at table three. The meat is dark and rich with a touch of funk, the skin thinned out and shrunk tight over it. Almost translucent.

When I butcher squab, I remove the legs and head, keeping the back on the rest of the bird to support it as it dries. Then I cure the legs with salt and herbs from our garden. I slowly cook them in chicken and squab fat reserved from stock until the meat is tender. I roast the head and split it, then season it with house-made vinegar and salt.

I put two squabs into a room-temperature pan breast side down with oil and bring up the heat. In a moment, the oil will be ready to smoke, and I will cool it down with butter, flip the birds over, and baste them with the frothy fat until they are golden. Just as I place the squabs in the pan, I look over at the guests. A man and woman, young, definitely on

a date, are looking at me and smiling. I smile back and then baste the birds. I feel things when this happens.

I know I am in the right place at the right time. This is why I am here.

At the end of their meal, I clear the couple's last course. The young woman stops me and says, "I so appreciate what you do. It must be really amazing to do this."

"Yes, it is," I say, like so fast, zero hesitation. I think I become a little red. Sometimes I even get a little teary when people thank me like that. I add, "Some days are long days, but you saying so makes it worth it." Truth.

They both bat their eyelashes. They say, "Thank you," and I say, "Thank you," and walk away.

I can hate all day up and down the bullshit that comes with running a business, but I can't deny that I'm probably not employable by anyone but myself. I certainly can't deny that when people appreciate what we've put together, me and my team, it all becomes worth it.

Even the unemployment paperwork. Even the dick jokes.

Some mornings, I pop up like I've awoken from a nightmare. My eyes red, bags underneath, pupils dilated. Everything compounds, like the collapsing of a concrete building floor by floor: my list for the daytime prep, emails to answer, paperwork, store run, calling the IRS, checks to sign. I hear myself through all of it, the subliminal hum of creativity and inspiration, me teaching myself while dreaming how to fix that dish. *What was that?* I try to recall. When I do: *Right. Try to dehydrate it before freezing it. Also add more acid to the*

sabayon because the aeration dilutes the flavor. I send myself an email. My life is a series of reminders to myself; if I don't send them, I will never remember, and it's just another collapsed floor with everything smashed in between.

It's eleven on a Saturday morning. I didn't have time to make coffee at home, so I carefully drive to the coffee shop in my neighborhood. Leaving the house before coffee is dangerous. I have about five hours of sleep in my system, but today is going to be a long one. My eyes might seem gentle, but they hide an under-caffeinated woman who generally hates the world. I shake off the kinds of bad thoughts, homicidal and suicidal thoughts, that have become so much rarer due to my life being beautiful now. I won't diminish that—even though sometimes I feel like I'll never be caught up with anything.

I cup the four-dollar cortado between my palms and sip it. My thought patterns begin to shift and become a bit lighter. The caffeine helps. It's all going to be OK. I can do this.

By the time I get to work, my cortado is about done. I scoot in past my staff, smile as they all chime, "Good morning." A lot of them are good kids, and my goal is to teach them to the best of my ability, even when I want to yell, and show them how to be good. How to be a success. I obsess with them over the food we make, our service, how we get better, drilling it all into their brains. At least, I drill it into their brains that this is how one successful chef and businessperson thinks. Even on the days I'm hating myself and I don't feel like a success, I have to pretend like I do and encourage them to keep getting better—explain to them how things work, why something emulsifies or sets, what to do to cure the meat or preserve the berries.

A good day for me is when my prep list reads:

Make chicken skin "snacks"
Practice new vegetable ash ramen noodles
Make milk ice
Decide on themes for next year

A worse day for me is when my prep list reads:

Call State
Health department inspection
Pay insurance
Get someone to repair back door
Pay myself?

I love testing ideas, random inspirations—those last-minute ideas I think up right before a busy shift, which I know drive my staff insane. I obsess over age-old techniques and how to perfect them. I'm not sure if people realize just how difficult it is to craft some of the foods and preparations they take for granted. I also love this part of the day, when all the adrenaline rushes through me, when every particle of me is filled with creative energy. It's like a high, or maybe it's just the residuals of the lysergic acid from high school, one too many little squares dissolved on my tongue.

Sometimes I write an entire menu in a single sitting. Sometimes I put this energy into a new dish or food item, and if I can squeeze it in and complete it just before service, I can set it in the daylight to photograph it. There is no better time of day to take a photo of food than midday. If it's a little cloudy out, even better.

Any achievements I've earned as a chef are the result

of long hours and constant obsession. Each second of the day, I'm calculating, learning. I watch everything and take mental notes. Being a chef is being a teacher and leader, but for me, it's also the ability to not believe I need to know everything before anyone else. I learn from my staff too. I've learned things from the guys obsessed with drawing penises on every label and from the meek, doe-eyed students still in culinary school.

Someone at a table stops me: Where does my creativity come from? Also, do I sleep?

Yes, in fits. The creativity comes from everywhere. Sometimes it's a dream, sometimes a daydream. One of my employees once said she could tell if I was daydreaming. She said even though I might be awake and looking at what was going on, I was often disassociating with the present, as if I was actually just looking *through* everything. Sometimes she'd catch me in the act. "What are you seeing?" she'd ask. Oftentimes it was a composed dish that reminded me of the woods, the way a chanterelle will look sticking up from the ground. Or how it tasted that day my dad and I got caught in the sandstorm. Other times, though, it was just my dogs. Or it could have been something much darker.

When I'm making a new dish, I *see* the finished ingredients, the textures, the colors. I see it in the overcast daylight, just as if I were taking a picture. Light and dark colors, bowl or plate, all of it already there.

The inspiration comes from nature, like a walk through the woods. Sometimes it comes from a good home-cooked

meal, one I've had or always wished to have. Or a photograph by Signe Birck. Or plate ware, pottery, service ware. I can't go into a clay studio, garden store, antique store, Village Discount, or Salvation Army without spending money I shouldn't and coming out with a whole new set of menu ideas to match the plates.

A lot of it is pure obsession.

I'm not always nice in my kitchen. I've yelled, hollered like a coyote. Many days, I have thrown trays and food against the wall. Many times, I've picked on someone over and over for being too slow, too messy, too disorganized. Many times, I have joked with a mean spirit. I've behaved all those ways the big bad-boy/bad-girl chefs behave, but at the end of the day, if I've behaved that way, I feel ugly. *Why can't I be better?* If I am better, they will have to be better, and the ones who don't climb to the top with me fall off. Sometimes I remind myself of the people I promised myself I wouldn't be like. If I'm lucky, I realize it and make necessary apologies, and we move on. These days, it happens much less than when I first started or when I was still drinking.

Here's the thing: before I opened my first restaurant, the one thing I couldn't teach myself was management. Is there anything in life that can prepare you for managing others? This was something I'd never really thought about. What I'd thought about all those years was the food I wanted to cook. The ingredients I wanted to play with. The places I foraged. The time I wanted to spend in the woods collecting. The time I wanted to spend in my garden

nurturing all the vegetables and fruits. I thought about the stories I wanted to tell, how I wanted the food to look, what inspired me. I thought about the cookbooks I wanted to write. But I never, ever gave a thought to all the twenty-somethings I'd come to hate and love.

Little did I know they'd expect me to teach them things. Why didn't they know what I knew already, especially those who came to me with lots of experience? Lots of them bragged about their time working at fancy restaurants. Well, then why can't you make simple things taste good or redo something when it's not right? I thought we were all in this together. I was pretty good at managing myself. Where was their ambition? Their passion? What the hell was this? Then they also wanted me to remember when they needed time off, or when they could start, or when they needed something. Or they'd call off 'cause they were sick. Or they'd tell me they couldn't make something 'cause we didn't have eggs. Like, what the fuck? *Well, go to the store and get some more eggs.*

I opened Elizabeth on September 21, 2012. For the first year, at least, I was there every single day and night—at the end of the night, on my hands and knees, scrubbing the floor. Over time, for the sake of sanity, things shifted. My job began to evolve from being part of the prep staff and executive chef to being executive chef and business owner. Sometimes the transitions were hard for the staff. I could sense their resentment when I was no longer prepping with them and instead was telling them how to do something while I focused on managing the bills.

Those first few months, I had difficulty gaining the respect of my male employees. I'd been in kitchens with lots of yelling.

If it wasn't directed at me, sometimes I was yelling. And even then, in the few kitchens I ran before my own, there were usually only one or two employees. Then, with Elizabeth, suddenly I had a kitchen full of six-foot-plus males in their twenties drawing penises on prep lists, order boards, and the tape of their mise en place and talking about fucking everything. Did I mention the penises? Literally. On. Everything.

I'd try to engage by being raunchy too, or I'd just tune out and work in silence. On days when it all became too much—the jokes, the disrespect, the blatant inability to listen to what I wanted—I'd fly off the handle and become "the crazy woman." As a boss, owner, chef, teacher, errand person, disciplinarian, and all the other things I had to be, I was still expected to maintain my female dignity and smile, be even-tempered, be compassionate.

The only thing I was able to do consistently was work hard. I'd work even harder when, behind my back, I'd hear them say things like, "This place wouldn't run if it wasn't for me." One by one, they all weeded themselves out. They left so they could remain prep cooks or become pizza delivery drivers or leave the industry entirely, while I stayed to run my restaurant, fueled by their ignorance to push harder. Each time a new crew member came in, I was more able to say, "We don't talk that way here," or "We don't do that here," or "We don't yell like that here," or "I'm not going to breathe down your neck," or "I'm not going to babysit you," or "You have to be good because this is your job, but being good should be about your life."

In turn, my crew members were more able to say to one another and to new people as they came in, "Chef will fire you for that." They scared each other because, I guess, I scared

them, but it wasn't because I was trying to. It was just because I was serious about what I did. And even as a female who was even-tempered and smiling, I suppose I was still scary.

I continued to teach myself. I learned how to say no without feeling like I was being mean. I learned how to say exactly what I wanted without having to explain why it should be that way. As of today, I haven't found a drawing of a penis on anything in almost five years. I occasionally get a new person in who questions me in a way I don't like, and I recall the name of his last chef. If he is a male, I say, "If I was so-and-so, would you ask that question now?" If they do something atrocious, like stack meats improperly or label their mise en place incorrectly, and I know their last chef would not have had it, I ask, "Would you do this at so-and-so's restaurant?" It's all rhetorical. I know the answer. Most times, there's silence because I don't really want an answer and we both know what that answer is anyway. Either way, that question (whomever it may be directed to) always leads to one place—if not that day or week, definitely within that month: the door.

There is no question about who is in charge, and at this point, my gender has nothing to do with it. And when I get emails or posts on social media from trolls, I just roll my eyes. I used to care sometimes about that. I have always thought it was weird. Now I don't have time for it. I haven't read the comments on anything in a long, long time.

When you're a boss, you have to talk to people all fucking day long. It means a lot of people following me around as

soon as I walk in the door. Like, I just want to finish my goddamned cortado first. But there they are, asking questions, anticipating answers. A normal person might like this. I really think some people do like this, sometimes. But me—a chef and alcoholic, someone born shy, introverted— it's not good for me.

On any given day, I transform, moment to moment, from businesswoman to chef to mother to motivator to babysitter to counselor to teacher. It's exhausting. And I hate to say that because it makes me think of chefs who say things like, "If you're exhausted, you're not a chef," or "I'll sleep when I'm dead," or "I push through the exhaustion because I fear failure." Sure, yeah, bro. I'm sure this can be true—and maybe if I was only a chef every day, with a little teacher and babysitter combined since that's part of the role, that would be fine. But fuck them! How about that? Everybody can go fuck themselves! (Warning: this is me, being The Chef.) To do all these things is exhausting, but I do it and I will probably fall over and die doing it. One second, I might love everyone—employees, humans, the world. Then hours later, I'll be at home, leaning against the bricks of the garage, inhaling cigarette smoke so deeply you'd think I was begging for it to take me out then and there. I'm not afraid to say that I get exhausted and that I get sick of all the everything. But that makes me no less creative and no less a chef and no less anything.

I get caught off guard, not only at work but also sometimes at the end of the night, when it's just me and the wife in our bedroom. I look around and think, *How did I get to be*

here? How the hell did this all happen? Where are the adults? And why do I have to be one?

I become paranoid, thinking it's all about to go to shit. *How can I do this another day? Another season? And if my front-of-the-house captain comes up to me one more time and says that table wants their tartare course cooked up, I'm truly going to gut him instead of just imagining it.* Then suddenly, service is over and it was good and I'm congratulating the staff on a job well done and I feel good. We talk about our prep lists, place orders, try to relax a little. I remind them not to go out and be a bunch of drunks because tomorrow is another busy day and they need to be 100 percent present.

I wonder if we chefs are unfit for whatever a normal life is. I believe I am.

2:48 a.m. I get out of the shower and lie in bed, too fucking tired to shave my legs, which look like tarantulas are crawling on them, and somehow even now I can't stop working. I have a long day of babysitting tomorrow because some days that's what being a chef feels like, giving these kids a last chance before jail or selling insurance.

I open my sticker-covered laptop and go to our website to double-check that the photos we have up look right and relevant, and then I see the menu page. *This is so wrong, and I have to micromanage every fucking thing all the fucking time. Why can't I just give someone a task and they do it right? He prints the same goddamn menu every single day, and I just want it to be correct on the site, and somehow there are wrong words,*

weird hyphens, and why the fuck wouldn't he look at the changes after he's given them to the webmaster?

I send an email, no punctuation, at 2:50 a.m.: "please i dont want to micromanage but can you just have the webmaster put the same menu up as the menu we are currently serving then next time check what it says." Then, I just do it myself.

On another day, I get an email: "We want to know your favorite Thanksgiving Day recipe. We want to include you because we don't want to hear from all guys, you know?" So there's that—the gender thing. Do they really want to hear from me? Or do they just want another voice, any woman's voice, trying to balance it out? Does it matter? Do they think I'll be more interested in responding so I can help their cause, to split up the difference? I don't respond.

Most days, I'm too busy to think about my gender or my sexuality. I'm fine being in the middle.

There were definitely times in the beginning of my career when my gender and soft-spoken nature may have closed some doors or made it more difficult for me to advance or get the things I wanted—like investors. When I was twenty-three, I knocked on the front door of Il Mulino on Dearborn. An older man opened the door.

"I'd like to pass along my resume," I said.

He scrunched up his crooked, snobby nose and said, "We don't hire females."

What in the motherfucking fuck?

I'd hear about different male chefs, certainly with less business sense and less credibility than me, closing deals with the shake of a hand over a beer or two. Meanwhile,

at Elizabeth, I started with mostly home equipment in my kitchen and a used stove that came with the space until I could afford better. I had to save up for the proper refrigeration. We had a home fridge and a drop freezer. Jesus Christ, sometimes chefs show me their stoves, and they cost more than it cost me to open my entire fucking restaurant.

Bro-ish handshake deals over cold beers have not been my experience. My experience has been that to get the things I've wanted, I've had to work my ass off. The same applies within the walls of my restaurant. Occasionally I have an employee come through who has worked at another establishment, one led by a male who has come up in the industry in a different way. Maybe he's got rich parents or super-fancy investors. This employee might say of his former boss, "He says you fuck your fiscal partner." Or, "He says that you don't know what you are doing." Or, "He says your restaurant is weak"—OK, whatever that means. In an industry full of dick jokes and macho fronts, this is *my* restaurant. I'm grateful. I have no need to talk negatively about my colleagues, even if I don't particularly like them. I usually say, "That's interesting— they were kind to me the last time I saw them."

Process. I began to obsess over bread and baking. Life-changing, again. Even after getting our first Michelin star in 2013 (and every year since), I still felt like I needed to accomplish more. For a while, I felt bad for my staff because all I could talk about was bread, fermentation, and crumb structure, but I suppose they reaped the benefits. All of us also gained about fifteen pounds.

I started working toward opening a bakery before I even really had a good foundation in bread, before I even knew I *wanted* a bakery. I had a good brioche recipe and a few other yeast-dough recipes but no solid bread-making foundation—I mean making that yeasty, funky, custardy, hard-crusted, naturally leavened bread. I had been tinkering with naturally leavened starters but was still unaware of how addictive it could be. You can make a good loaf of bread and fuck everything up the rest of the day, and you'll still have a good day.

I heard a story on NPR about a coffee shop somewhere in San Francisco that sold toast. I thought that sounded nice and simple, like I could do something like that. So I booked a trip to go to this toast place, and to eat bread at what everyone says is one of the best places for bread: Tartine.

While I was out there, I researched bread-making on my own—walking the streets of San Francisco, up and down the hills, the houses like wedding cakes—that way, I knew what I was trying to achieve. I pursue the standard and then I immerse myself in the details to teach myself how to make something that will be aimed at a level of craft and quality imperceptible to some who come into my restaurant. (Some of those customers, I have learned from my staff because I don't read it, will later post on Yelp that they "weren't blown away." *Suck a dick.* Yelp is like a ten-ton dick. Boinking you on the head. Boink. Boink, boink.) Luckily, the majority who come to my restaurants recognize that level of craft and quality. I pursue it for myself first, then my staff, then for those who love it.

When I came back from San Francisco, I had an idea. I pulled a loaf of our brioche out of the oven and said aloud

to my staff—like I do with so many ideas—"What if we just added sugar to this brioche recipe, cut it into doughnut shapes, then fried them?"

"Hell yes," was the unanimous response.

Here comes the process: I take the same brioche recipe, reduce the butter and milk content a pinch, add a touch more sugar and some vanilla bean, and then beat the hell out of it in the stand mixer. I put it in the refrigerator for up to forty-eight hours to let the flavor develop. It's a mixture of natural leaven and yeast. When I take it out, I roll it on a lightly floured surface to about a half-inch thickness, then punch out circles. I let them rise at room temperature for an hour and a half, then put them back in the refrigerator to cool so that I can handle them without deflating or stretching them.

But this method didn't just appear to me the day I asked my staff that question. First, I went out and tried doughnuts everywhere people told me the doughnuts were good. Each day at work, I tinkered with a recipe. When I found something I liked, I tested its sturdiness: Can it be frozen? How long can we refrigerate it? Can I give this recipe to someone else to execute? Each time I found an error, I went back to the drawing board. I filled scrap paper and whole notebooks with recipes, crossing them out one by one as they failed. I turned to science, researching how yeast and dough and resting and rising and temperature all play a crucial role in doughnuts.

After about eight months, I had a dough I liked. A bit sturdier than what I wanted, but a recipe I could give to others to execute. The key was the temperature of the doughnut—it had to be a certain temperature before it went into

the fry oil—combined with the amount of time it had developed, risen, and rested. Really, the recipe's development was just a bunch of practicing and falling all over myself in the meantime trying to figure it out.

Finally, though, I had it. The best doughnut. Ever. My good friend, the food writer Jason Tesauro, says eating my doughnuts is like going down on a cloud. That's pretty super. *Holy shit.*

That day, we all stood around the kitchen pass. My apron was covered in flour, my hair aromatic with fry oil. I dipped the doughnuts in a whiskey glaze. Everyone smiled. *Yeah, that's pretty fucking good.* Months upon months of talking about doughnuts, making doughnuts, redoing doughnuts, getting mad at the people making the doughnuts, sending angry texts when I couldn't find the doughnuts. All of it paid off in those first couple of bites. I knew that when we opened this bakery—which didn't even have a name yet—it was going to be great.

Also during that time, I developed our naturally leavened sourdough. We had begun to feed our starter with a very yeasty, champagne-scented whole wheat that gave off that really sour funk you look for when making bread. I spent a year developing the recipe for the bread. It started with a cattail pollen roll, and by the end, we had a bread that was thick-crusted, sour, full of glutinous strands of crumb, and gorgeous enough that food writer Terra Brockman told me it was the best bread she'd ever had outside of Brittany.

I took my new knowledge and began to build more breads and flavor profiles from it. I pored through books and

read up as much as I could on yeasts. I taught myself how to collect wild yeasts and then turn them into bread starters.

Making a good loaf of bread can entirely change my mood. When it's executed correctly, I can be in a good mood for the entire day. On another day, if it doesn't work, I'm back to thinking about what might have been wrong, feeling worthless, sad. That's it. That's how it is. My sense of self and happiness, a lot of the time, resides in the execution of my food. If I can't get these things right—like bread and dough-nuts—then I'm not being the chef I want to be.

It's almost noon. I pick up my handwritten prep list and pour myself a second cup of coffee. I walk through our dining room—some of the crappy ceiling tiles have shifted out of place from the wind. People are enchanted by our "tin" ceiling tiles, but really, they're plastic tiles that fit into a dropped ceiling, mimicking tin, covering the debauched ceiling above. A couple of months ago, it fell in and there was a whole bunch of water damage all over the place. Elizabeth was not in the best shape when I got her, but I put in a lot of work to make her appealing. It's been a long road and a lot of fixing things.

I pull up our curtains and tie them together to let in what daylight I can. I turn on the lights. Before I get in, my staff often works with only the kitchen lights on and the dining room dark.

"How can you guys do this," I ask, "and not fall back asleep?" I have to remember, again, that they are still in their twenties.

I check in with everyone on their prep lists. I ask them if they need anything. I discuss a bit of what is on my agenda for the day, what I'll be working on in the kitchen or in the office or off-site. I reflect on the night before, what I think could have been done better, what I did and didn't like about plating, service, the preparation of the food. I tell them about my dreams without mentioning the dream.

I look at Mikey. "We have to add a bit more lemon juice to the sabayon."

"Yes, Chef."

I look at Nathaniel. "Dehydrate the egg yolks a bit longer before they go into the freezer."

"How long, Chef?"

"Until they're right."

"Yes, Chef."

I want them to trust their instincts. I want them to be good cooks. I want them to be chefs themselves someday. That's the whole point, right?

Over time, I've learned there are many things that need exact recipes and many things that are dependent upon touch and taste. Some fruits are sweeter at their peak. Some tomatoes are tarter. It just depends, and these kids have to first develop and then trust their own judgment. I try to encourage them to make decisions for themselves—as long as they run the basics past me first. Like, go get eggs if we are out.

I go to our back kitchen and sit down and open my list. A baker who's been with me for five months now says, "Hi, Chef."

"Hi," I say. "So on the list today for you, I have test doughnuts. Let's test out the croissant recipe in the new

oven. I really think the heat of this oven is going to give us what we are looking for."

"Mm-hmm," she says, slightly smiling and nodding in agreement.

"Plus it would be great for us to have doughnuts this week. We haven't made them in a while, and we should make sure we have got it down."

"Yes, Chef."

I head to our office to change my shoes and put on my prep apron, where I am greeted by my office guy. "Good morning, Chef."

"Hi. Morning." I'm still feeling salty about the website.

"So you know, I contacted JJ and he's updating the website."

"Thank you," I say and walk past him. I unlace my boots and put on my clogs. "When we change menus, can you double-check things like this so I don't have to come across it? It would be super helpful."

"Yes, Chef."

How do they all have that response? Everyone. Part of it is great. But every once in a while, I want them to have a better response. I'm still searching for what that might be. Sometimes it doesn't feel right. Like those moments when suddenly I'm stunned and I get that glazed-over look and think, *How did I get here?* When it's unbelievably amazing and frightening as hell.

I head downstairs. I fold and tuck a towel into the side of my apron. I put my scissors in my back pocket, put my tweezers in my breast pocket, and clip a Sharpie to my apron. I wipe up the table where I'm going to set down a thick wooden cutting board, and I think to myself that chefy-bro

phrase, *Make it nice.* Sometimes you just can't escape it, even if you really, really, *really* want to.

I'm going to teach myself how to make *xiao long bao.*

April 8, 2016. I listen to Alison Krauss. Her voice is like an angel giving you butterfly kisses on your ears. *Next best thing to playing and winning is playing and losing.* I close the record player and sit in silence.

Later, my hand trembles like a beat hooker's as I drag on my cigarette and cry my eyes out. It's past noon and I'm still in my pajamas, hair a mess. I hope to God my mother, who lives in the apartment below me, doesn't look out the window. For one, I don't want her to see me smoking; for two, I don't want her to see me looking like a hooker in heroin withdrawal, trembling and feeling like I'm dying inside.

I had just finalized my decision to close Bunny, my bakery, which had only been open four months, but which I'd worked on getting ready for two years. Five minutes before, I had posted on all my media outlets that we would be "closed until further notice." The press was so fast to respond; it's annoying. I understand it's their job, but suddenly they all wanted to be my friend, all, "Well, if you ever need to talk . . ." It makes me cringe. I generally don't want to talk at all, and the last thing I wanted to do was talk about how terrible this felt. I loved Bunny, but I got mixed up with the wrong people opening it.

The day spirals. I can't crawl out. Instead, I try to set the living room rug on fire. I hated that rug. My girlfriend at the time, Jehna, had a Chihuahua that pissed on it every day. It

was an outdoor rug, made of some sort of jute rope. It collected dirt and little pieces splintered off. I really hated that fucking rug.

Seemingly possessed by demons with snake-slit pupils, I crouch down, grab the end of it, and light a match. I sit down against the wall, but there are no more tears. I just watch the flame.

It's a statistic that more women than men are arsonists. Turns out, I'm not an arsonist. I put the flame out. Then I sit there with nothing left to do.

January 20, 2017. I stood inside Kitsune a few hours before we opened. I held a framed picture of Barack Obama I had found in the office. I gently placed it on the shelf behind the bar, full of reverence and devotion. It's still there.

I was scared as shit. I opened Elizabeth on a real tight budget. We had more with Kitsune, but I was still so freaking scared.

It was like the time my mom, dad, and sisters took me to school on Halloween because there was going to be a haunted house in the rectory. I didn't look like I would have been a frightened little kid. Before we left, Elizabeth sat me in front of the mirror in the upstairs of our farmhouse. She squirted mousse in her hands and slicked all of my hair back. She took eyeliner and lit a match against its tip. While it was soft, she drew a widow's peak on my forehead. She brushed eyeliner on my cheeks, forehead, and chin like wispy strands of fur. I wore a black cap and pointed ears. I was a perfect little werewolf. I've got the pictures to prove it.

My own twist on the costume was to carry a deer skull I had taped to the end of a large stick. My family was enamored with my strangeness. My mom proudly told people the stick and skull were my own creation.

There we were in the chilly night, waiting outside the rectory, shivering. I really had talked myself into this. I was going to do it. I was going to go in like the big bad wolf I was, and I was not going to be scared. Maybe I'd scare the priests with my death wand. We got up to the front. I saw some of my classmates, but I didn't talk to them. I didn't really talk to anyone, even though people wanted to know about my cool costume. When it was our turn, suddenly I felt stuck in the cement of the steps. I didn't want to go in. Big tears welled in my eyes. My sisters asked if I was OK, and that was it—tears gushed down my face. The eyeliner ran until my whole face was just one dark mess. My dad picked me up, and we went to the car. My mom, the good RCIA member she was and newly experiencing Catholic guilt, did not want to show up and not support the school, so she paid the small fee and entered. After that, we all went home.

I'd started planning Kitsune before we opened Bunny. And then, feeling overconfident that I could handle all these small restaurants, I had no idea what I was up against with these real wolves and me just dressed up like one.

I was afraid I couldn't handle another small restaurant, undercapitalized by the time we opened because of setbacks. We had needed more money, and I didn't know how to ask for it. I got stuck being the little girl. *If I was a man, would I just say it? Shouldn't I know how to do this by now?* Delay after

delay allowed me to heal from the pain of losing Bunny but just added on more and more rent paid with no income.

I cried the morning I placed our forty-fourth president on the shelf. I cried for many reasons. Some good and some bad. I promised myself I wouldn't let us fail. I wouldn't feel like that beat hooker. I wouldn't set anything on fire. I wouldn't burn the place.

In 2018, Kitsune was named a best new restaurant by *GQ*, *Esquire*, and *Chicago* magazine, and it received a whole bunch of other beautiful accolades. We've landed in a pretty good place. We still struggle. We are still behind. I'm not trying to make this like every other chef memoir—you know the ones, like a big fat cum shot of douchery—no, I'm just trying to keep it real.

Chapter 15
Stories and Creativity

1986. I HELD OPEN *THE BOOK OF GNOMES.* I WAS BORN there—I knew it. The houses in the sides of hills. The mushrooms, goblins, deer, field mice, flowers, crockery, earthen tones. A pop-up book that was so captivating it took my underdeveloped brain and filled it with all sorts of dreams and ideas, as if it came through my eyes in winds of glitter and gold, filling me with notions of my future. Look at the book yourself and you'll see. It's the same as my restaurant.

I sat alone on the floor of Elizabeth's first apartment with Kristina's dad, Dean. They had just gotten married, and I was the flower girl. Torture. I wore the dress, but I had spiked hair. Everyone still told me I looked pretty, even though my two front teeth were gone. It was cloudy that day. There's a picture of me in that flower girl dress with all the ruffles and blue sash, my mouth like a prizefighter's, the spiked hair. My mom brought me my favorite pair of gray jeans and a sweatshirt for

me to change into once dinner was over at the reception. That might have been the longest I had worn a dress in all of my seven years up to that point. My mom took me to the bathroom with my bag of clothes, and everyone in there, knowing I was the bride's sister, begged me not to change. I wasn't interested. I wasn't supposed to be in a dress. I was supposed to be in that gnome book, among the mosses and wildflowers.

1988. Sometimes I'd spend an hour or so playing paperboy. Since we lived on a farm on a country road where people drove fast, we didn't have paperboys who rode bikes. I dreamed of being a paperboy myself someday. I collected newspapers, which I rolled up and tied. I rode my bike in the neighbors' driveway, since theirs was paved and ours was gravel. I threw the papers every ten feet or so, and when I was done, I would stand my bike against the mulberry tree, collect the papers, and start over again.

I found lots of ways to keep busy. I suppose my parents appreciated it. This was another thing: I stacked up fifteen pieces of drawing paper. I drew a character on each piece. I used scissors to cut them out. I taped their necks and limbs to make them sturdy. I lined them up against a wicker toy box in my room. Keeping busy.

I was one of the dolls. Damon was my name. I had four brothers and five sisters. Our parents had passed away, and our two oldest siblings took care of us. We were a very rich family because my oldest brother built a virtual reality video game in which you got to be an avatar and enter the game by going into our backyard, which was under a large glass

dome that covered about four acres of land. The game had five worlds to choose from: Mars, Desert, Los Angeles, New York City, Everglades. You put on a helmet and glasses, and once you entered the dome, you were part of the world. You had to find clues to take you to a safe house. Once at the safe house, you got clues to what you did next. Basically, you needed to protect the world from destruction. This was Damon's family, remember, not mine. I was young when I made this up. *Mad Max* was my inspiration.

I had a book that listed the personality of each of my family members, along with their age and birthday, whether they were in a relationship, and what their boyfriend or girlfriend was like. Everyone was straight because I really didn't know anything about gay people.

My hair was brown and curly. I kept it fairly short but not too short. I had the bluest eyes you ever saw—so blue they might have been a window to my brain. All the girls liked me. I only liked one, though. Her parents had named her after Janis Joplin. But Janis didn't like me. She liked my twin brother, who had blonde hair and blue eyes and was more of a jock—taller, stronger, with bigger muscles. He wasn't necessarily cuter than me—it just depended on your type. Every night, I thought about Janis. My sisters gave me advice. They taught me how I should behave with girls, how to tell if they liked me or not.

1994. My cousin was born some months after me, and we sort of grew up together. For a long time, it was almost like we were twins, both towheads, but I was always a little lankier. Her name was Mandy. Mandy had a sleepover. There were

about ten of us there. It was dark and I was in a large reclining chair with one of her friends. I can't remember who it was. She was pretty, though. In my mind, I just pretended I was Damon as she snuggled against me.

I was starting to feel like I was too old to be Damon anymore. As I made more friends and spent less and less time alone, I couldn't just be him like that. I looked around and everyone else was lying all over each other, braiding each other's hair, painting nails and stuff, so this seemed like it might be OK. I put my arm around her, and she looked up at me and smiled. Snuggling. I was Damon. *This would be normal if I were him.* Maybe she was thinking the same thing. Maybe she thought I was Damon too. Or maybe she was being Damon and I was just me. I kept thinking I could kiss her. I kept thinking it would be OK 'cause she was looking at me like she wanted me to do something like that. But it didn't make sense right then. It was feeling forced. I was forcing myself to be him. It didn't feel like it did when I was alone. Like I was all busted into pieces. Maybe I should have just been happy that she was snuggling on me 'cause she was pretty. She smelled like strawberries but not fake ones. Green strawberries. So there I was, all busted into pieces because there was a girl in my arms, and she knew I was me, not him. I didn't kiss her. I didn't do anything any different from what any of the other girls were doing. I was still one of them.

1996. It's like a centrifuge. Every freakin' moment of your life, spinning you around so fast and pulling you right to the bottom. Everything just firing right down to the hard

pavement. I remember that time, lying in bed, shivering under my covers, "LA Woman" echoing off the bones inside my skull, just waiting and waiting for the acid and the hangover to go away. It sort of never left. I still see tracers. Fuck driving at night. I do it, though—all Day-Glo and pixelated. My friends are like, "WATCH WHERE YOU'RE GOING!" And I'm like, *What? I haven't even been here. I was with the aliens.* I wasn't, though, but maybe I was, 'cause I had no idea where I was going either.

2003. My professor's glasses always slid down to the tip of his large nose, but the round Rudolph-like bulb kept them from crashing to the floor. He had gray curly hair around the perimeter of his head, and the fluorescent lights of the classroom beamed off his shiny naked scalp. He told me he liked me because I didn't hold anything back when I was writing. When I turned in my stories, the kids in the class asked me how I thought of what I was writing.

I said, "I'm just writing about people I know. It's not necessarily them, but most of it is."

I included Kate and Chloe in some of the stories, some of the twisted-ass boys Kate had dated, some of them hillbillies or acid freaks or ruddy-faced drunkards with fast cars. They would be the protagonists. I included my dad and sisters. My dad and the way he'd chase boys away, shooting guns or pretending like he was going to rape them 'cause they had long hair or something.

Like in Virginia Woolf's stories, someone was always grieving. Someone was always in love with someone else.

And there was always someone in love with someone else who didn't love them back. But the stories were also fantastical and dystopian—the world was ending or had ended. Some character was usually able to travel through time or see into the future. Sometimes they could read people's thoughts, or animals could talk.

After Elizabeth died, I wrote a novel, a collection of short stories, and two books of poems. Writing was the only way I could deal with the grief. And drinking. Thinking about stories helped take my mind off things. I would walk to the train and think of what would happen next. Everything I saw, I wrote, imagining how it sounded. Everything became part of my characters' lives and stories. I needed to escape. Sometimes I thought dying might just be better.

2010. I sat at my desk. At 1 a.m. I took out a pen I used for sketching, along with the same brand of sketch notebook I used for writing. I spent the next two hours constructing my first menu.

Amuse:

> *Hibiscus tea, salmon roe, and white chocolate foam*
> **The guests will drink this out of a champagne glass through a bubble-tea straw.*

Course 1:

> *Salad of green tomato sorbet, peas, pea shoots, dried morels, and tiny herbs*

Course 2:

> *Sassafras-brined and grilled octopus, root beer, and cherries*

Course 3:

 Shrimp, avocado, and coconut
 *This will be tempura-battered and fried. It will be served
 as a single bite on a stick.*

Course 4:

 Seared scallop, shellfish custard, and saffron risotto

Course 5:

 Gobstopper of egg yolk, fig, and green peach, with lamb
 heart glazed with a peach reduction
 *The gobstopper will be a cured egg yolk center, wrapped in
 fig gel, dipped in a crispy peach shell.*

Course 6:

 Smoked paprika–cured pork belly, with ham consommé
 and tiny potatoes

Course 7:

 Kumamoto oyster ice cream, cornbread shortbread cookies,
 and mignonette gel
 Serve this on an ice block.

Course 8:

 Coriander and citrus cake, lime curd, cola nut, and vanilla
 ice cream
 Flavors of Coke

Mignardise:

 Chocolate consommé and rosewater shot glass
 *The rosewater shot glass will be actual seasoned rosewater
 frozen in shot glass molds.*

I escaped into menus just as I escaped into stories—by the
fiction I wrote or the paper dolls I drew and then became.

By the time I opened Elizabeth, my menus told stories too. About what I grew, where I went to forage, how I preserved something, how I procured raccoon for sausage or deer bones from hunters, how I speared and decapitated frogs.

Chapter 16
Good Ol' Indiana

IF YOU ASK ANY GOOD OL' INDIANA BOY OR GIRL, they'll tell you they've either gone giggin', know someone who gigs, or know someone who might have a gig if you need one. I know 'cause I'm a good ol' Indiana girl, and I'm there a lot. It's a place I love and hate, that Midwest full of scary people but beautiful, tall, wild grasses. I'm a wild grass too, I suppose. One of the scary ones too.

A frog gig sort of looks like Poseidon's scepter. It's got anywhere from three to five prongs, with what appear to be fishhooks at the ends. Sometimes the apparatus has a female side so you can screw your own pole into it if it doesn't already come with one. That's the recommended way—get just the head so you can decide on your own pole length. Try using something like a painter's pole, something sturdy, yet pliable and adjustable. That way, if you are trying to get a frog that's far out into the pond, you have a good amount of

range. Finding the pond is key—you gotta find a nice clean one. But almost any pond will do. The legs on the frogs you gig are going to taste sweeter than any other frog legs you've had before. If they're from Indiana frogs, they're sweet like candy. Getty says, "Sweet legs, baby."

Most frog legs come to the United States in frozen one-kilogram bricks. The frogs are grown on tilapia farms somewhere overseas. They have a shitty life and they taste fishy. But our Indiana bullfrogs taste as if a crab and a chicken had a baby: juicy, sticky, fleshy. They're big too. The biggest one I've gigged was sixteen inches long from head to toe. Maybe that's an exaggeration, but not by much.

Cuisses de grenouille, the hind legs of frogs, is a dish people associate with French food. The legs are poached in butter with a sauce of peppery nasturtium, blended with chanterelles or some other forest mushroom, like morels. Morels taste just like steak (that's what my dad says).

Once you've found your gig and a pond, you have to wait until it's the perfect night. There are lots of perfect nights in the Midwest, when it's warm. In the colder months, the frogs bury themselves in the muck of the pond. Their bodies match the temperature; they can get near freezing and they become dormant. As soon as it gets warm, they thaw and come to the surface. They grow fat on the good, rich protein of insects. Frogs like to congregate right where the water and the land almost meet, and they prefer taller grass as the dew starts to form at the tips and the sky darkens. If the moon is out and the temperature is about twenty degrees less than the inside of your mouth, you're bound to hear their deep guttural croaks. Sometimes the dark night

sky romance gets to them, and you'll see them fucking or spawning.

You'll need a headlamp to find your way and a flashlight to stun the prey, like a deer in headlights. You have to catch their eyes with the flashlight. The best way to do this is to have your wife, girlfriend, boyfriend, husband, best friend, new friend, or whoever come with you to be the stunner. Their job is to shine the light in the frog's eyes. You'll have the gig.

The stunner can also carry the frog bag, which can be as simple as a garbage bag, unscented. Canvas might be better. But you'll need something that can be closed at the top. Frogs are very resilient critters.

When I first went frog giggin', it was with Getty, that beautiful boy from back home who gave me my first drink. I put my frogs in a cooler, and he kept his in a garbage bag. I had also stuffed all my pockets with milkweed pods and gave him about ten.

"These aren't going to kill my family, are they?"

"No, I promise." I handed him the pods, my hands full of their sticky milk. "Use your best tempura recipe."

"Yeah, I got a good one."

"Dust them with a little cornstarch, then dip them in the tempura and fry them. I swear the seeds inside are attached to thin, silk-like fibers, and they melt."

"That's crazy," he smiled. Getty's face was big now, the way men's faces get when they age. He still looked a bit like the boy he had been but also as if stress had aged him.

"It's like cheese. Even has a little funk to it. Think of it like a jalapeño popper without the heat." Getty and I had grown up and eventually become friends. He didn't remember any of those first encounters—not the drinks, the playing ditch, any of it.

When I got back to Elizabeth, I took the cooler out the bed of my truck and set it on the ground. I opened the lid, sort of terrified about the instructions I had received about ending their lives. Getty had casually instructed me to cut off their heads.

"Yeah, but what if they croak or something?" I had wondered.

He had reassured me that this would most likely happen, along with their maybe even jumping off the table where the massacre would take place.

One of the frogs jumped out of the cooler. Its little guts poked out on one side, just above its right leg. *Resilient as fuck.* I had hoped they all might just have been dead by that point. Here's the deal: if you love frogs more than you love to eat them, don't add frog giggin' to any of your bucket lists.

When you gig frogs, you have to be quiet. If they sense your presence, they will jump from land to water one by one, perfectly timed to the sound of your encroaching footsteps. Soon as you find your quiet rhythm, you want your stunner to shine the flashlight about five to ten feet ahead of you. You'll be looking for sets of tiny iridescent pearls. These are their eyeballs. You'll see them. Sometimes, if you're at a smaller pond and your flashlight is strong enough, you can shine it all the way across and see them. Once you've got them in your light, focus on the closest one. Slowly move

forward, instructing your stunner to direct the beam straight into its eyes. At this point, you've got two options.

One: Position yourself behind it, maybe as close as you need to be to make sure you get the gig right through its back, right above the *cuisses*. You'll drive the gig far into it, pushing it into the soft shoreline. You'll crouch down to get the leverage you need to pull it up, also taking the mud, algae, leaves, spiders, and whatever else might be attached. Pull those off, keeping in mind that there might also be some guts and whatever else was pushed through by the gig. Be strong. Put it in your bag, and move on to the next.

Two: Do everything the same as in option one but without the gig. With this method, the "hand grab," you've got to trust your speed and be willing to grab the critter with your bare paws. It feels slimy, firm, and wriggly all at the same time. Grabbing it with your hands might be the more humane way to catch a frog. But then you've got to figure out how to kill it anyway. Frogs are much livelier when they haven't been gigged, of course, and it takes some steady hands to chop off their heads.

The night I came home with the gigged frogs in the cooler, I put them in the freezer until the pond water had crystallized between their bodies, but I could still snap them apart easily. I flattened them out along the cutting board and with one slice, severed one's head. Then I flipped the body around and sliced through the joint connecting the hind legs and back. I held the legs up with one hand and, with pliers in the other, I cinched a loose flap of skin around the middle of the body. Like a pair of skinny jeans, the skin rolled down the length of the body into a little thin strip, and when I

pulled it off, the webbed toes turned inside out. If you reserve the skin, maybe set up an Etsy account, and make frog-skin change purses.

Dip the frog legs in salted ice water after you skin them. You should also clean up a little of the sinew around the muscles, but that's not entirely necessary. If I were you, I'd dust them in a little flour seasoned with salt, pepper, and a little lemon zest. Heat a cast-iron skillet, add butter, and sear them till they're a little golden on each side. It won't take them long. Then eat. The Beer Barrel, the pub near where I grew up, used to serve these. So drink beer when you eat them. I'll just have lemonade, though.

Chapter 17
Things That Matter

2015. My dad still has the same jagged way of driving: he guns the motor, then *bam*, he hits the brakes. We shift forward. The rifles in the trunk thud against the back seat. On instinct, I duck. We are going to target practice. Maybe this is all he intends to do, shoot the target, sight in the rifles. But I'm here for the stories. I don't get the chance to spend a lot of time with my dad. I like the Q and A. He's got an A for everything. I get that from him. We've never had a strong bond, except maybe back before I was big enough to know I was a girl. Sometimes I feel awkward around him; I've never been good at being his little girl. At least I haven't felt like I have. I do know, though, that he keeps every single thing that's ever been written about me—if it's online, he prints it out and keeps it in a box. He gives them all to me.

Anyway, this feels pretty good and normal. I ask how far does a shotgun shoot? Why is the soil sandy here? What

happens to the bullet once it goes in the air? Answers that maybe I should know, but I don't, like, have you ever tapped maple before? How do you get sugar from beets? Why did Grandpa buy that farm? He answers, half speculating, I know. He tells me that the farm came with mineral rights on the deed, and that rarely happens anymore. That the Polish guy about a mile south of Grandpa's farm drilled for oil and now has two wells. It's poor-quality oil but good enough to buy a new Cadillac every year. But Grandpa never wanted to drill for oil. He says, "Grandpa always said, 'I bought this farm to farm on it.'"

The range is closed. Gated and chained. Instead we drive to Grandpa's farm. I loved Grandpa. Of all my grandparents, he was the one that you wanted at your birthday party—sweet, generous, loving, excited, and playful. I'd demand paper money from him, and he always gave me a dollar. The day Grandpa died went like this: my dad was sitting on the back porch at the claw-foot table, which was usually spread with newspapers and dried tomato seeds. It was the morning and he was crying. I was young, maybe five, not very understanding of how I was supposed to feel and definitely not accustomed to one of my parents crying. Maybe I was supposed to cry? My dad took me in his arms then because he knew I loved Grandpa or maybe because he was faced with death, and his own life was flashing before his eyes. Maybe he realized, at that moment, that someday this was going to happen to him. He hugged me tight and I felt my chest constrict, and he whimpered that Grandpa had died. I felt his tears fall in my ear and down my neck. And I yelled for him to put me down.

I should have told my dad I loved him. I should tell him now.

Instead, I'm sitting in the car, having trouble staying off my phone. I came here to be with him because I do realize our lives are just that short and fast. I can't fucking stop working, though. And part of me thinks, *He was gone, maybe he deserves it.*

He starts to talk about the leaves changing colors. I put my phone down. We drive east on Route 10, among the sandy hills, burgundy amaranth, corn, propane tanks, and small houses, with the woods in the backdrop and a fat wild turkey and sandhill cranes in the meadows. He asks if I remember when he hung ham in the garage and it'd be "hard as this," and he taps the steering wheel.

"Yes," I say, almost tasting the smoke.

Grandpa's farmhouse looks abandoned. It's a trilevel house, built in the '60s. White. The siding is falling off. The roof is torn in some areas. There are a few remnants, like a child's tractor and ball in the yard, but the grass has grown heavy. I remember Grandpa's hair, thick like that. At least a summer's worth of yard work untended.

"Doesn't look like anyone lives here," my dad says. I just want to go in, walk that sandy path to the birch trees, look for mushrooms, pick dewberries from the hedges. But you can't love it unless you hate it. Like on Sunday mornings there, *The Lone Ranger* on their black-and-white television, Uncle Georgie sleeping in his basement room. If he wakes, I run.

My dad backs out and we drive a little farther up the road, hoping to find someone to ask about the white house. My dad swears he has an uncle Andy who just died about six months

back who might have known something. I ask why I don't know this uncle. I've rarely heard him mentioned before, and I certainly didn't know he lived out here. My dad says he's weird.

I ask, "Like child molester weird, or likes to fuck goats weird, or hermit weird?"

My dad chuckles uncomfortably. "Just weird." Right then, I think my dad is a victim but of what, I don't know.

We stop at a green house. My dad and I get out. He drives a long black Ford Taurus, maybe from the early 2000s. He's got on khakis and a polo shirt. I have on a beanie, my hair tucked up in it, somewhere between male and female, arms covered in tattoos, wearing hiking boots and a flannel. If you didn't know us or if you were like a lot of the squatters in Medaryville, Indiana, you could certainly think we were DEA or FBI agents and not answer the door. But this place is too cute. They have a nice porch, wind chimes, old tractor seats painted primary colors and refurbished into chairs. But alas, no one answers. We get back in the car and think. A little out loud, a little quiet. We drive down about a half block, and a man appears along the road.

The man is maybe sixty. He smiles big. People in Medaryville don't always have all of their teeth, but this one does.

"We're looking for someone who might know the Regans' farm. That white house up the way there." My dad points and the guy squints.

Then a school bus comes along and the guy says, "Here's the answer: Carol Tanner, she drives that bus. That green house is hers. She drove me to school, my kids to school, and this little guy now." A young boy materializes and suddenly jumps in the man's arms. "This is my grandson."

The school bus pulls into the driveway of the green house and Carol Tanner steps out. My dad says hi and introduces himself. "I'm Regan. My father used to own that white house up the road. I'm wondering if anyone is living there now?"

"Nobody's lived there for at least five months," she says. She's got wild gray hair.

My dad talks about how he had to sell the house back in '91 when his mom went to a nursing home and then passed. He had planned to retire, but his daughter died and he adopted his granddaughter and had to keep working to get her insurance 'cause her dad didn't have any. On and on. I'm not much of a talker myself, but I understand how you can get going with certain people, especially when they might have a clue to the past.

Carol asks my dad his age.

"Seventy-five going on seventy-six."

"Us too."

She disappears into the house for a bit and my dad keeps talking. When she comes back out, she gives him a slip of paper. They say a few more things before he comes back to the car and Carol Tanner goes inside again.

My dad shows me the paper. *Rick Peterson 219-769-0001.* "He lives up north," he says.

"Why do they say 'up north,' as if they're southerners?" I ask. I'm being an asshole.

"Well, Chicago has a south side and a north side, don't it?" my dad responds. OK.

"Let's go back. If no one is there, let's drive up. They said they remember Grandpa. That he was always out there doing something," my dad says.

He is satisfied. He wants so badly to have anyone today remember. The remembering brings his dad back to life. I know. That's how it happens. It makes the dead real again, knowing that another person knew them when they were alive, too. We think, *Was it all my imagination? Did I really have a grandpa? Did I really have a father? Did I really have a sister? Was that even in this lifetime?* Someone else remembering makes it all real.

This is hard for my dad. We are so alike; I can see it today. I have had this recurring fantasy, since we moved out of the farmhouse, that someday I'll get it back. I'll buy it back and move there and live the rest of my life there. After Elizabeth died, my longing for the farmhouse became stronger; if I could get it back, then she'd be back too. If I could get it, I could turn back time, and we'd all be there again. The shag carpet, the '60s décor in the bathroom, the cast-iron owls by the fireplace. My sisters would all be there, and then all the dead would be right there. All of them.

My dad must have this fantasy too. If he could get this farm, he'll get his dad back. I put the property address in my phone, hoping it might be for sale—or better, foreclosed.

My dad says, "Maybe the guy who bought it from him died. He never lived there, he only rented it. The man had a younger brother, but who even knows?"

Then I can see he starts to spin.

"I could buy it back," he breathes.

This whole time, I can see the emotion caught in his chest, face, eyes, and I'm all over it.

"I'll help you fix it up," I say. "We can farm it. We can hunt there. We can pick mushrooms. We could get this land

back. We could drill the oil wells. I could outfit it, build a pond, fill it with bluegill, crappie, catfish, bass. You can fish. I could have a restaurant there."

"Hmphf," he says. I know it won't happen.

At the white house, we head to the back, where the yard is worse than in the front. I see the big propane tank I used to climb on as a kid, pretending it was a horse. We park just where we always parked, right before the path that led to the woods. To my left is a big old oak, its acorns scattered across the old drive. The last time we were here, I could just barely see out of the passenger window, but now it's like I was never away, as if this place is still ours. I can see my grandpa on his tractor, slowly pulling the dried corn toward us.

I look at my dad, and he looks deep past my shoulder into the field, and I know he sees him too. Grandpa's big handsome head with all his hair, wearing his overalls and big boots.

We get out. From the back, you can see right through the back porch door into the second level. It seems empty. I get nervous.

"What if it's full of squatters? Meth heads? And right now they're all taking cover because they think we are the police?"

"They have junk everywhere. I can't believe how over-grown this is. Grandpa would have never let it get this way." My dad is upset. His eyes seem to get tinier every year as the skin around his face swells and wrinkles, but I can see they are wetter than usual.

At this moment, I realize I have to be the strong one. I go over to check the barn door. I walk through the sand and

up a short incline to the big red barn. The structure of it is still quite beautiful, but the whole area is full of junk: an old stove, papers, plastic bags, beer cans, clothes. It's as if they made their own garbage piles right here, rather than taking it anywhere or having it picked up. I try the knob on the side door; it's locked. Just beyond are the old pig stalls and more junk, vines growing across chicken wire, hubcaps, a tricycle, an oil can.

"Push it," my dad says.

I do. Nothing.

"Try the big door," he suggests.

I go to the front where the large sliding door is, but there is a padlock. I look at him. Before I walk back to the car, I say, "You want me to kick this open?"

"No, just get back in."

"Why? No one is here. We can explore."

"Just get in the car."

I get in the car.

"I'm going to call the owner. We'll come back after I do," my dad reassures me.

"But no one is here. I'm serious. Plus, we have guns. Let's get out and explore. Let's go look at those abandoned cabins in the woods. We can get some sheep's heads. The weather is perfect."

My dad shakes his head. "Carol said that some people were trying to make drugs back there in the woods, and they got caught by the cops."

We stare at the path that leads to the thick woods. I couldn't have been more than waist high the last time my dad and I walked this path. I remember the warm sun on

my tiny arms and ball cap. How my shoes filled with sand as I shuffled down the path. We liked to pick blueberries and dewberries along the way. I had a little basket. I would weave my arm through the brambles and thorns. The blueberries were plump and covered with a thin layer of yeast. The ones I picked never made it to the basket.

My dad told me, "Kids are the best mushroom hunters because they are closer to the ground."

The first time we had ever gone hunting for mushrooms, I was wearing cowboy boots, jeans, and a red zip-up hoodie. And my Incredible Hulk underwear with the pee hole that my grandma had convinced my mom it was OK for me to wear. All these years later, my boots were brown with lassos etched along the ankles and calves, and I was still wearing superhero undies—Wonder Woman, with no pee hole. The hoodie, the jeans. All these years and I still dress like I dressed when I was just a wee lad.

That first time, though, the oak and birch leaves were all sorts of warm colors and scattered across the ground. They shattered beneath my dad's footsteps and crackled beneath my tiny boots. The weather that day had been warm but with a razor blade's cut of a chill. My dad had pushed his glasses up his nose and brushed away the hair that was hanging in his eyes when he told me, "Remember, we're looking for the ones that look like sheep heads."

At the base of the largest, oldest, sometimes even dead trees, we would find them. The smell of sheep's head mushrooms is like nothing else. It's so rich and pungent, with wood, earth, and nutty aromas, that it could be mistaken for a cutlet of veal. That's what my dad says, but when does a

cutlet of veal taste like wood, earth, and nut? I repeat what *he* says, though, when I tell people about this mushroom. We picked the leaves and sticks from between the petals of the mushrooms. Potato bugs scattered from the layers. Under those trees, I marveled that we were collecting our food, and I was smitten.

We decide to head home. My dad and I can't stop talking about the treasures to be had there or what we could do with it now. Oil rigs. Hunting tours. A shooting range. Tapping trees. Farming. Building cabins. Our ideas fly out the car window and settle over the farm fields as we speed west on Route 10.

We go to Grandpa's house every spring and fall now. We stop in the path, the trees tall above us. The brush is overgrown and my dad shakes his head each time he looks at it because that's not at all how Grandpa would have kept it.

He points at the corncrib. It looks like the frame of a big old garage. He says they'd drop corn in there from the grain elevator and used it for feed for the hogs and cattle. Now the cornfields are overgrown as well. The remaining stalks are fossilized at knee height, and their little corn ears litter the rows.

"That crib's made of beechwood," he says. "It's a strong wood, never seems to rot."

I'm mystified. I love this place and at the same time, I feel like we are both on edge. I start to speculate about what my dad is thinking or feeling.

I am scared, really. Next to the corncrib, there's a trailer that's fully fucked up, door slung open, insides torn apart. It might have been a nice camper at some point, but now it's a

haven for muskrats or coons, black mold and shit. I'm sure at some point it made for a good meth lab or even worse, a place to tie up children. That's where my mind goes. And what I'm afraid of today is someone scary being out here.

I think, *Here I am with my dad, whom I've I always thought of as big and strong, and he is big and strong but he's old now,* and that's hard to think about. He can't protect me now. Each time I walk deeper into the woods, looking for morels, he calls me to come back out, and I'm thinking it's because he's got the same bad thoughts that I have. It's chilly and my nipples are hard and I should have worn a better jacket, and if there are bad people out here, they are going to know exactly what to do to me, especially looking like the tomboy that I do.

So there we are. I'm afraid, and I think he's afraid too.

But when we leave that day, it ends like our other days out here—with all the possibilities. We are dreamers.

Chapter 18
The End

WE WERE IN THE BACK OF MY JEEP. IT WAS A CHILLY night. We had the seats down. I had on a hoodie and a beanie and a long army-green coat wrapped around my body. Anna wore a fluffy sweater and a slim, long, tan wool coat. She looked smart. I looked like a criminal. We were watching a movie.

It was our second date and too early to be heading to one another's houses, maybe too early to be staying out with each other for so long, longer than we had planned. She said she didn't know how to date someone like me. She was used to going out to bars and having terrible conversations while the person on the barstool next to her talked over her about themselves and asked all the same old questions; it just became monotonous.

But this was different. Our conversation was strange, and it made her laugh. She had laughed when I said, "Well,

if we're not going to one of our houses, I have *Star Wars* downloaded on my computer; we can put the seat down and watch it in the back." This seemed weird too—like I could be a weirdo. I made sure to tell her, though, that I wasn't going to try anything weird. She looked at me quizzically, almost like she was disappointed.

Then I told her I didn't think she'd be there anyway, if I wasn't who I was. Not that I thought I was something great, but before I had a restaurant and was adorned with the shining Michelin star and all that nice media, I was just some lady obsessed with mushrooms, the woods, catching frogs, and things like that. Which might make me sound like some kind of little kid.

She gave me another weird look and said, "I also think you're beautiful and smart."

That was nice, so I settled in my head. Even though I'd said I'd try no funny stuff, I thought I might still try to kiss her.

So there we were. The spaceships zoomed all around the screen, and we rested our heads against my book bag, and she put her head on my shoulder, and I put my arm around her. Her face was bright blue from the glow of the screen, and I'd never seen someone look so pretty by the light of a computer. She looked up at me a couple times, but I still didn't kiss her—not till the movie was over and we had nothing left to do.

If you don't know Anna, when you see her, you'll know who she is after I tell you: she's the one with the heart-shaped face and the dimples that look like they were carved there. Her eyes are the color of the sky or the grass or the

gray of the lake or whatever color her shirt is. Her eyes are sequins. She comes in colors, like a rainbow.

I didn't say that—that's Mick Jagger. Little did I know that when Elizabeth, Kristina, and I were driving through the thick Florida heat, the tiny tan Mustang rattling, top down, and we learned Kristina could sing every word of "She's a Rainbow" from her little two-year-old mouth, I was calling to Anna through the universe. I shouted, "She comes in colors everywhere," every time we played the Rolling Stones tape on repeat, flipping it over each time it came to an end. I was calling her to me, through the universe, just like fate, and she was coming to me. Eventually, exactly what I wanted.

I shut my computer and leaned toward her, and she leaned toward me. Then we kissed.

Well, you know how that goes. We ended up getting married. Twice. Once at the courthouse with the judge as our witness on October 31, 2017. The second time was with all our friends and family as witnesses, a whole big group of people we loved, and not even all of them. We wrangled everyone for an entire weekend at a summer camp. It was like the pop-up dinners we do sometimes, but never so big as this. It was the best day. I know that's a cliché, but I think that's what a good wedding is with a good partner: it's the best day. She'll tell you that too.

Before Anna, I had been bumping along the bottom of what sort of felt like a day in, day out kind of hell. Or at least the second or third level of hell. But I had made my choice, and that was to reign in hell rather than serve in heaven.

I know that all sounds dramatic, but feeling down is a whole bunch of things to a whole bunch of different people, no matter what the outside looks like.

I could blame a million different things. The day Donald J. Trump was inaugurated, I picked up the restaurant linens from the laundromat on Damen Avenue. Michelle Obama was on the television screen, the embodiment of eloquence. I couldn't look at the televisions hanging from the dropped ceiling. I began to cry instead.

I could blame the business partner I had run away from, causing me to leave my beautiful little Bunny Bakery behind.

I could blame all the other things that were bothering me, even though a lot of them were first-world problems and I knew my life was really pretty great. What the fuck was I doing, getting these jewel-like vegetables, like you see piled at Whole Foods, and these beautiful farm-fresh meats? What was I doing, preparing food so that it cost so damn much and was only affordable to an affluent clientele, while others starved? Have you seen the children in Yemen? I felt so fucking pretentious.

I could blame all the guys in my industry giving me shit for being me. Or just men in general. Inequality. The women who belittle and hate other women—maybe they're the worst of all.

I hated myself for feeling this way. My sponsor reminded me to attend more meetings, sponsor other women, get out of my own fucking head. The head is the worst place to be. This is how I was feeling. All I could think about were these things. I questioned myself, my career, all the choices I had made. Every day felt like too much.

—

That night in the car, after we kissed, I apologized for my episodic ranting. I really hadn't talked a lot at our first few dates. She knew who I was from things she had read. I told her I liked to play Legos when I had free time, and I teased her a little, which she liked. But then I had comic book–like bubbles of word bursts—dark, brooding, damning things. Cursing the world, shit like that.

Maybe she liked my rants. I mean, of course she did. We're married, for Christ's sake.

"Look," I said. "I'm sorry if I was being a drag with all the negative shit."

"I think it's funny," she responded.

"It's truly not that I hate people. I think I love people, maybe too much sometimes. I just feel let down. That's all." I looked at my hands. "Rather than saying I'm sad, I say I'm angry. But really, I'm just sad."

I drove her home that night thinking I wouldn't see her again. That I'd probably said too much. I tried to shrug those thoughts away while I listened to the Grateful Dead. Anna had made fun of me for that, but my love for the Grateful Dead transcends time. Elizabeth loved them. We saw them in concert together; she'd eaten mushrooms and her eyes had bugged out like big emeralds. We listened to them on the porch of her old Victorian house in the Georgia countryside, among the fireflies.

I imagined myself alone again. Driving somewhere far away, the continent whirling along my windshield.

I parked my car and stood near the garage. I lit a cigarette

and felt hollowed out. There were just a few stars in the sky that I could see. *Damn city lights, smog, and shit.* I could hear the planes flying in and out of O'Hare. You know, all the people coming home or going somewhere exciting. All the things you ordered online, shipped in from China. I thought of child laborers with arthritic, tired little fingers. I thought about the images of hungry kids I'd seen on television when I was a kid: their protruding ribs, skeletal legs and arms. I couldn't understand.

My phone dinged. I pulled it from my back pocket, expecting something like, "This isn't going to work for me."

It said, "So on Sunday, if you're free, want to come to my house and play Legos?"

It was late Friday night now.

I said, "Yes. Sounds super." She thought I was being sarcastic, but I was being real.

We got married seven months later.

I was like the black sand from a volcanic island, all black, slipping back and forth between the water and the bedrock, a bunch of tiny black pebbles. I gave Anna a black diamond ring when I proposed. I put the ring in a Lego box for her to find, knowing that whenever that night came, she'd empty the box and find the ring. She cried.

I think I said, "Don't cry. I'm serious, why are you crying?"

She said something like, "Is this for real?"

And I said, "It's not a joke."

I told her the ring was black like my heart. She thought that was funny. But I was sort of serious.

—

Maybe on our eighth or ninth date, I was lying in her bed, watching the rain hit the moonlit bricks of the neighbors' apartment building. She said she hoped that we wouldn't hurt one another. I said that everything ends with hurt. Everyone ends up hating each other, sometimes for the very things they once fell in love over. She told me that was bullshit. She told me that sometimes people can love each other forever. I told her to prove it.

Anna didn't save me from anything. She didn't stop me from being a black rock. Sometimes you just wake up. I woke up. She helped me do that. But all the changing I did in the meantime, the opening up, that was for me. I felt like I wanted to become better. It's not that I was bad. I needed my mind rearranged. You can still hit bottom, even without the bottle.

Anna proved to be just as wacky as I am. She's the one who asked me to play Legos. I put the ring in the box for the *Star Wars* set of Legos.

We are still building it.

I told Anna about my silver bullet trailer dreams—me and the dogs at the edge of the world somewhere: red dirt, mountains, blue sky, container garden, twinkling lights, neon stars, sliver of moon, wolves, coyotes, bears, trees, all that. She was in.

She asked me, "What about Elizabeth?"

And I said, "What about it? I'll burn it." But now that's just a running joke. I only tried to burn anything down once, and that was my apartment. I really didn't like that rug.

On our fourth date, Anna told me when she got married, she wanted an armadillo cake like the one from *Steel Magnolias*. I didn't think she meant when she got married to me. But on our wedding day, we had an armadillo cake. I cut off its tail and swung it around in the air. On the Friday before the wedding, we played *Star Wars* under the stars on a big screen so everyone could see what was so romantic about it.

I always wanted to be a carny, remember? We bought that silver bullet travel trailer and drove it out West. We drove it out East too. We've driven it to the North and even a little through the South. And none of it's too scary for two girls sailing along the black pavement, the heat rising up like cobras for miles, with nothing in front of or behind us. We're not afraid, even with our bumper sticker that shouts, TED BUNDY WAS A REPUBLICAN, because we travel with two huge dogs and one really, *really* mean little dog. And we've got bear mace. We weren't even scared when we camped in North Dakota, without another gay person, let alone a person of color, within miles. Truth is, people are nice. And people are good to us. Maybe it's 'cause we are girls. Maybe it's 'cause we are nice-looking. Maybe it's 'cause we are nice. Maybe it's 'cause they're afraid of dogs. Maybe it's 'cause I sort of always set the bear mace within eyeshot. Maybe it's 'cause, of all the people we judge, thinking they might be hillbillies, it turns out *we* are the ones who are hillbillies.

You can't ever really take the Indiana out of the girls. Anna is from Bloomington. You can't take that out of us. We

set up a blue fence each night around our trailer and make it like a little double-wide under the neon, star-pocked sky. Out there, it's like millions of neon dots—you really know you're in the Milky Way when you're out there. You can even see the cosmic showers go by on their way to nowhere.

And I realize while looking up, with all of our clothes hanging over the fence to dry, that this place is a good place. We are all outside in the dusty landscape, and we are our own little carny tribe. It's good.

Dimples and I are buying a farm. Soon. No worries, you'll be able to visit.

Epilogue

8:15 A.M. IN THE BATHROOM. I PEE. GEORGE, THE BIGGEST dog, busts in. He uses his head like a battering ram. I have just started the coffee. An actual pot this day, not the powdered kind. I hear it in the kitchen. I smell it. I see in my underwear around my ankles that I've started my period. One of my first male employees told me he used to track my period each month, and a sign that I was going to start was when I would fire someone.

I asked him, "Does someone really get fired from here once every month?"

He laughed, "Yes, Chef."

"Fuck," I said in disbelief.

I haven't fired anyone in a long time. There's no need. Like I said, the ones who need to go sort of finish themselves off on their own.

I open the medicine cabinet and pop a Lexapro, biotin,

magnesium, B12, D3, omega-3, CoQ10, and a few other things. I do my skin care regimen, using only by-products from the restaurant. A face mask of buttermilk, honey, coconut, almond skins, bee pollen, clay. A cream cleanser with beets and chocolate. A toner with tomatoes, cucumbers, mushrooms, aloe, and turmeric. A face cream with shea, coconut oil, grapefruit peel, and cedarwood.

I swear my eyes are becoming crossed as I study the new wrinkles that now crease my face. I know I'm about to make a big change. I'm not sure what it is yet, though.

Well, I do know but I'm not going to tell you.

My mind is racing. I get on my knees. God forbid Anna sees me do something like this. I fold my hands in something of a praying shape over my heart. I whisper, "Spirits, gods, guardian angels, nature, all the beauty in the world. Please help me be kind and loving today. Please help me to think before I speak. Please help me to understand my family, wife, colleagues, and employees. Help me to be tolerant of and empathic toward others. Help me be open to change, free of judgment, and full of love for the good of humanity." I stop when I hear a light knock on the door. It's Anna. I quickly get up.

"One sec."

I make the sign of the cross—muscle memory—as fast as I can muster. "Thank you, God, help me in general, and keep me away from the devil's drank. Catch ya later."

The day begins.

Acknowledgments

THANK YOU TO MY SPONSOR AND THE PROGRAM OF Alcoholics Anonymous; without these, I'd be dead.

Multitudes of gratitude to everyone who is and is not mentioned in this memoir. You are all important and you know who you are. Katie K., Daaimah M., Anna L., Sarah F., Melissa F., Caitlain F., and Mo W. If I had entered a story for every person and event that shaped my life, this book would have never ended. There are women and men in my life to whom I am eternally grateful. Who taught me to be wary of judgment, let go, and keep going.

To Tonya P., who saw me through many life changes and was a cheerleader for me, no matter what. Still is.

To Brooke S., who was there when I opened my eyes.

To my good friends Kate M., Jill T., Kelly C., and my cousin Mandy K. We had some really good times.

Thank you to my past employers, those who taught me

what to be like and those who taught me what not to be like. I'm not the best but I'm trying every day to be good.

Thank you to my employees—past, present, and future—for keeping me from really burning the place. To my favorite, Shannon Martincic—without her at the helm during my writing of this book, it would have taken far longer than it did. She's my rock.

To my mom, dad, sisters, and the farmhouse. It turns out I was exactly where I was supposed to be this whole time.

Thanks especially to our guests, those who return year after year, menu after menu, do all our things, and keep our lights on. You keep me going.

Obviously, to Doug Seibold and Agate Publishing.

Lastly, most importantly, to my wife, who is a constant ear for all my grievances. She's kind of an angel. And goes along with all my big plans.

About the Author

Author photo: Jeffrey Marini

Iliana Regan is a self-taught chef. She is the founder and owner of the Michelin-starred "new gatherer" restaurant Elizabeth and the Japanese-inspired pub Kitsune, both located in Chicago, and Milkweed Inn, a farm and bed and breakfast in Michigan's Upper Peninsula. Her cuisine highlights her midwestern roots and the pure flavors of the often-foraged ingredients of her upbringing. A James Beard Award and Jean Banchet Award nominee, Regan was named one of *Food & Wine*'s Best New Chefs 2016.